AND WITH YOUR SPIRIT

ALSO BY VIRGILIO T.J. SUERTE FELIPE

_____

English Mass for Filipino Catholics: The Meaning of the New Words of the Holy Mass

The Lord's Supper, Eucharist, Mass . . . What's In A Name? The Names of the Eucharist in the 2002 GIRM

Theo Week 2004: Love, Compassion, Solidarity in a Globalized World (co-edited with Fr. Fausto Gomez, OP)

Theo Week 2003: Life, Hope, Holiness (co-edited with Fr. Fausto Gomez, OP)

Theo Week 2002: Faith, Violence, Values (co-edited with Fr. Fausto Gomez, OP)

Universal Prayers of the Faithful for Weekdays of Advent and Christmas

Panalangin ng Bayan sa Panahon ng Adbiyento at Pasko ng Pagsilang

Guidelines on Building New Churches (edited)

Cardinal Sin and the February Revolution (edited)

AND WITH YOUR SPIRIT
Appreciating the New Words
of the Holy Mass

VIRGILIO T.J. SUERTE FELIPE

authorHOUSE®

AuthorHouse™ LLC
1663 Liberty Drive
Bloomington, IN 47403
www.authorhouse.com
Phone: 1-800-839-8640

Published by AuthorHouse   07/02/2013

ISBN: 978-1-4817-1283-5 (sc)
ISBN: 978-1-4817-1285-9 (e)

Library of Congress Control Number: 2013902099

This book is printed on acid-free paper.

Imprimatur:

✝

Most Rev. Deogracias S. Iñiguez, Jr., D.D.
September 30, 2012

Nihil Obstat:

Msgr. Geronimo F. Reyes, J.C.D.
September 21, 2012

INSIDE PHOTOS
The inside photos were taken by Angelica J. Regalado except for the photo of the statue of the pregnant Virgin Mary on page 58. The statue is from Fatima, Portugal, and owned by Dr. Rodolfo and Mrs. Nora Tabila. Dr. Tabila took the photo of the statue.

Contents

To the Memory
of
Father Anscar J. Chupungco, O.S.B.

Acknowledgments

I would like to express my heartfelt gratitude to:

Most Rev. Deogracias S. Iñiguez, Jr., D.D., Bishop of Kalookan, for his *Imprimatur* and valuable comments and suggestions;

Most Rev. Oscar A. Solis, D.D., Auxiliary Bishop of the Archdiocese of Los Angeles, for generously appearing in the photographs;

Rev. Msgr. Geronimo F. Reyes, J.C.D., Judicial Vicar of the Metropolitan Tribunal of Manila, for the *Nihil Obstat;*

Rev. Fr. Raymond Vicente Ma. Decipeda, MMHC, Pastor of Holy Family Parish, Artesia, California, for granting me "leave of absence" from The Center for Faith Formation;

Dr. Rodolfo and **Mrs. Nora Tabila**, for giving me a job in the U.S. that afforded me the precious time to write this book;

Angelica J. Regalado for the photographs;

Alex A. Meñez, Aloysius A. Meñez, Evelyn P. Ribas, George and **Melanie Del Carmen, Julian A. Quinabo, Lance Kayser, Noel G. Asiones**, and

Raynato M. Manansala for reading the manuscript and their valuable comments;

Dr. Loida P. Constantino, Dr. Violeta M. Anorico, Dr. Virgilio and Mrs. Antoinette Panganiban, Angelica J. Regalado, Corazon T.J. Suerte Felipe, Esperanza M. De Vega, Leticia M. Guzman, Marilou M. De Vega, Nerida R. Ancheta, and **Virginia P. Francisco** who have all helped me directly or indirectly in finishing this book.

The ultimate acknowledgment belongs to **Father Anscar J. Chupungco, O.S.B.**, whose name has been "synonymous with liturgical inculturation" (Francis, 2000, xii). As my teacher and dissertation adviser, he has taught me to study liturgy historically, theologically, and pastorally. He received a copy of the manuscript of this book in September 2012. Unfortunately, he did not see this book printed because he had passed away on January 9, 2013.

Abbreviations

CCC	Catechism of the Catholic Church
CSL	Constitution on the Sacred Liturgy
DOL	Documents on the Liturgy
EDE	*Ecclesia de Eucharistia*
PF	*Porta Fidei*
GIRM	General Instruction of the Roman Missal
ICEL	International Commission on English in the Liturgy
SacCar	*Sacramentum Caritatis*

Introduction

In his homily on the Solemnity of Pentecost on May 19, 2013, Pope Francis shares his thoughts on the working of the Holy Spirit with three words: *newness, harmony,* and *mission* (http://www.vatican. va/holy_father/francesco/homilies/2013/documents/ papa-francesco_20130519_omelia-pentecoste_ en.html). We can concretely apply these three words to the recent experience we have had regarding the changes to the Holy Mass. We believe that the Holy Spirit is behind the *new* translation of the Roman Missal which is a sign of *unity* in the Church in the midst of its diversity and which inspires its members to *go* and *proclaim* the faith celebrated in the liturgy.

But as we get used to the new words in our responses and prayers of the Holy Mass, many of us, to this day, are still wondering why changes have been introduced in the first place. Although we are getting familiar with the new expressions, many of us are still stumbling over "And with your spirit," "consubstantial", and "enter under my roof".

It is important for us to understand the new translation because it is the new way of participating in the celebration of the Holy Mass (cf. Francis in *With One Voice*, 2010, 55-85). The dignity of our common priesthood is most solemnly exercised through our active participation in the Holy Eucharist. And we can fully benefit from its fruits, if we have "a good understanding of the rites and prayers" (*CSL* 48).

In his Angelus Message on June 26, 2011, Pope Benedict XVI, now Pope Emeritus, said that the Eucharist "is the Church's most precious treasure". It is like a diamond ring that a husband gives to his wife as a sign of his deep love. If the husband is drafted into the army, the wife will surely see to it that the diamond ring is protected in a safe place and always kept clean while waiting for the return of her dearly beloved.

As Christ's Bride, "the Church has received the Eucharist from Christ her Lord not as one gift—however precious—among so many others, but as *the gift par excellence*, for it is the gift of himself, of his person in his sacred humanity, as well as the gift of his saving work" (*EDE* 11). As Pope Benedict XVI says, "The sacrament of charity, the Holy Eucharist is the gift that Jesus Christ makes of himself, thus revealing to us God's infinite love for every man and woman" (*SacCar* 1).

Christ gave this "diamond ring" to us, his Church, and left it to us how we should take care of it and protect it. In other words, Jesus Christ gave us the essential core of the Eucharistic Sacrifice; and the Church has supplied the external elements of the celebration "based on her experience of the Risen Lord and the outpouring of the Holy Spirit" (*SacCar* 37).

While waiting for the return of our Lord Jesus Christ, we have taken care of his "diamond ring" and protected it in a book called *Missale Romanum (Roman Missal)*. Its cover, design, and language have changed in the course of time, but the essential core remains the same.

When Pope Benedict XVI received a copy of the English translation of the third typical edition of *The Roman Missal* on April 28, 2010, he instructed us the gentle and effective way to keep our "diamond ring clean":

> The opportunity for catechesis that this time presents will need to be firmly grasped. I pray that in this way any risk of confusion or bewilderment will be averted, and the change will serve instead as a springboard for a renewal and a deepening of Eucharistic devotion all over the English-speaking world (Vox Clara Committee, April 28-29, 2010).

The Purpose of the Book

This book was written to provide a catechesis or "an *education in the faith*" (*CCC* 5). I am sure that you will ask, "Do we not have enough resources about the new English translation of *The Roman Missal*? What makes this book different from all the books and other catechetical resources that have been published?"

As an ordinary Catholic and a perpetual student of liturgy, I have been zealously following the preparation and the full implementation of the third typical edition of *The Roman Missal*. After reading the books published and the websites postings (including the blogs) and listening to the workshops and catechetical homilies about the changes to the Holy Mass, I deeply feel that the reasons given for the changes and the meaning of the new words in our responses and prayers are not adequately explained.

I have confirmed this in the workshops I gave in my capacity as Director of the Center for Faith Formation of the Holy Family Parish in Artesia, California, and in my private conversations with parish leaders and ordinary Catholics. To this day, many Catholics are still asking why changes have been introduced to the Holy Mass. I could not count how many times I have been asked about the meaning of "consubstantial".

This book explains the substantial reasons for the changes in the third typical edition of *The Roman Missal* and the meaning of the major changes in our responses and prayers of the Holy Mass.

How This Book Will Help You

This book consists of three chapters and two Appendices:

- Chapter I uses a *historical* approach in explaining the new English translation of *The Roman Missal,*

- Chapter II provides a *pastoral* catechesis on the new words,
- Chapter III deals with a *theological* or doctrinal explanation of the Holy Mass, and
- The two Appendices present prayers before Mass and prayers after Mass.

Chapter II is the heart of the book. To situate our responses, the subunits of each major part of the Holy Mass are first identified and briefly explained. Then it focuses on the new words in our responses by providing:

- a catechetical exposition of their meaning by analyzing their Latin origin and referring to the related portions of the Bible, the *Constitution on the Sacred Liturgy*, the *Catechism of the Catholic Church*, the teachings of Blessed John Paul II, Pope Emeritus Benedict XVI, and Pope Francis; and
- a spiritual and moral link with our life.

Two expressions of the Priest are also included: "The Lord be with you" and "The mystery of faith." Our reply to the greeting and our acclamation to the announcement of the mystery by the Priest are better understood if the greeting and the announcement are also explained. Our "Amen" to the Eucharistic Prayer also deserves some explanation.

References are integrated into the main text of the book. Abbreviations have been used for some of the primary sources. Specifically, references to the *Documents on the Liturgy* (*DOL*) are to marginal numbers, while references to the *Catechism of the*

Catholic Church (CCC) and other Church documents are to paragraph numbers. In the absence of paragraph numbers especially in the case of secondary sources, references are to pages.

Finally, the new English translation of *The Roman Missal* offers us the opportunity to delve more deeply into what we say and do at the celebration of the Holy Mass. This book aims to help in the efforts to avert the confusion which has been expressed by Pope Benedict XVI in connection with the introduction of the new changes to the Holy Mass, "I pray that in this way [i.e., catechesis] any risk of confusion or bewilderment will be averted."

Chapter I

HISTORY AND REASONS FOR THE CHANGES

Faced with the changes to the Holy Mass, many Catholics are surely asking, "Why introduce a new translation? We've been used to the prayers and responses for several years." In order to understand the recent changes, we need to look back and briefly go over the history and the reasons for the new translation.

When did we start celebrating Holy Mass in English?

When my wife, Lucille, and I together with our three children, Maria, Topher, and Angeline, came to the United States in June 2004, I called for a family meeting. I explained that we had to adjust to our new situation. We agreed, among others, that, while we continue to talk amongst ourselves in our own Filipino language, we are to speak English when we meet or eat together with other people.

Similarly, when the Church saw the changing times of the twentieth century, Pope John XXIII called for a general meeting or an ecumenical council. The Fathers of the Second Vatican Council discussed and decided on the necessary adjustments beginning with "the Church's most precious treasure," the liturgy. The Church agreed, among others, that while "the use of the Latin language is to be preserved in the Latin rites" (*CSL* 36 §1), the Conference of Bishops "is empowered to decide whether and to what extent the vernacular is to be used" (*CSL* 36 §3).

This opened the door for the native language of the people to be used in the celebration of the sacred mysteries of the Church. The Vatican has permitted the Conferences of Bishops to translate the Latin prayers and responses into the native language of the people (cf. *DOL* 913). Translations into the vernacular, according to Pope Paul VI, "have become the voice of the Church" (*DOL* 787).

Translations into the vernacular, according to Pope Paul VI, "have become the voice of the Church" (*DOL* 787).

By this historic move, the Church has revived her ancient practice of using the language of the people in proclaiming the Good News and worshipping the Lord from "Jerusalem . . . to the ends of the earth" (*Acts* 1:8). The early Church spoke Aramaic (Hebrew) to the Jews in Jerusalem, then Greek to the People of God in Constantinople (now Istanbul), and eventually Latin to the faithful in Rome (cf. Pecklers, 2003, 1-4).

The Conferences of Bishops of English-speaking countries established on October 17, 1963 the International Commission on English in the Liturgy (ICEL). Its main task is to translate the Latin liturgical books into the English language. Currently, there are eleven Conferences of Bishops that make up ICEL: Australia, Canada, England and Wales, India, Ireland, New Zealand, Pakistan, the Philippines, Scotland, South Africa, and the United States of America.

ICEL's English translations of the Latin liturgical books have been zealously received by the Catholic faithful. The first English translation of the Latin Mass appeared in 1969. We began to understand the prayers and responses of the Holy Mass. Consequently, we actively join in the singing. We attentively listen to the readings and prayers. We consciously respond to the Priest's greetings, announcements, and exhortations.

Why a new English translation?

To be candid, when the new English translation came out, my initial reaction was one of resistance and opposition. I found the new guideline used in the translation, *Liturgiam authenticam*, as insensitive to the cultures of the local Churches. But as I investigated the reasons for the changes, I began to appreciate the new translation. I saw the bigger picture.

After forty years, it has been observed that the Eucharist "is celebrated as if it were simply a fraternal banquet" (*EDE* 10). The sacred and solemn character of our worship seems to recede into the background. Thus, despite the lively liturgy introduced by the first wave of vernacular translations of the Holy Mass, Church members are still "longing for transcendence, stirring up in their hearts a desire for an intimate, personal relationship with the Triune God" (John Paul II, *Ad limina*, 1993, 2).

Also, "it has been noted that translations of liturgical texts in various localities stand in need of improvement through correction or through a new draft" because there are "omissions or errors which affect certain existing vernacular translations" (*Liturgiam authenticam* 6). We will see some of those "omissions" in the 1973 English translation in the next chapter of this book.

Moreover, following the guideline that "texts translated from another language are clearly not sufficient for the celebration of a fully renewed liturgy" (*Comme le prévoit* 43), ICEL did not only translate, but also composed new texts in English. One example of a new composition in the 1973 English translation is the familiar acclamation: "Christ has died, Christ is risen, Christ will come again."

Today, the Church wants to emphasize the spiritual or contemplative character and doctrinal dimensions of the Holy Mass by "rendering the original texts faithfully and accurately into the vernacular language" (*Liturgiam authenticam* 20). As Blessed John Paul II said:

When so many people are thirsting for the Living God (Ps. 42 (41): 2)—whose majesty and mercy are at the heart of liturgical prayer—the Church must respond with *a language of praise and worship which fosters respect and gratitude for God's greatness, compassion and power.* When the faithful gather to celebrate the work of our Redemption, the language of their prayer—free from doctrinal ambiguity and ideological influence—should foster the dignity and beauty of the celebration itself, while faithfully expressing the Church's faith and unity (Cf. John Paul II, *Vicesimus_Quintus_Annus*, 9 and 21) (John Paul II, *Ad limina*, 1993, 2).

> **Today, the Church wants to emphasize the spiritual or contemplative character and doctrinal dimensions of the Holy Mass by "rendering the original texts faithfully and accurately into the vernacular language"** (*Liturgiam authenticam* 20).

To accomplish such a great task, the Vatican Congregation for Divine Worship and the Discipline of the Sacraments:

(1) in 2001 adopted new guidelines for vernacular translations, *Liturgiam authenticam*, which "envisions and seeks to prepare for a new era of liturgical renewal" (7);

(2) in 2002 established the Committee of Bishops to advise the Vatican on English translations, the *Vox Clara Committee*; and,

(3) in 2003 reconstituted ICEL that produced the new English translation of *The Roman Missal.*

What is *The Roman Missal*?

The Roman Missal is that red Mass book which the Priest uses in saying or singing the greetings, acclamations, and prayers. *Missal* comes from the Latin *Missale*, which is the book for the celebration of the Mass (from the Latin *Missa*) that evolved in Rome. It basically contains the instructions, the Entrance Antiphon, the Collect, the Prayer over the Offerings, the Preface, the Eucharistic Prayer, the Communion Antiphon, the Prayer after Communion of every Mass throughout the Church year.

Like the *Lectionary* and the *Book of the Gospels* which contain the Word of God, *The Roman Missal (Sacramentary)* is also a sign of the presence of Christ. It signifies that Christ actually presides in the celebration of the Eucharistic Sacrifice through the ministry of the Priest who proclaims the prayers of petition and thanksgiving *ad Patrem per Christum in Spiritu Sancto* (to the Father through Christ in the Holy Spirit).

How did *The Roman Missal* come about?

When the first Christians gathered together to celebrate our redemption, the first book they used was the Bible, particularly the Greek *Septuagint*. With the fixing of the canon of Scripture (list of inspired books received by the Church) in the fourth century, subsequently the prayers for the Holy Mass also got fixed in the *sacramentaries*, the readings in the *lectionaries*, and the songs in the *antiphonaries*. From the ninth century, these Mass books were fused into one volume designated as *Missale*.

Following the liturgical reform of the Council of Trent (1545-1563), Pope Saint Pius V approved the publication of the *Missale Romanum* in 1570. He strictly imposed its universal use throughout the world. Four hundred years later, in 1970, following the liturgical renewal of the Second Vatican Council (1962-1965), Pope Paul VI authorized the publication of the first typical edition of the *Missale Romanum*. Its second typical edition appeared in 1975 and the third in 2000. The timeline below shows the corresponding years of English translations of the three typical editions of the *Missale Romanum*:

Editio Typica	English Translations
1970 *Missale Romanum*	1973 *Sacramentary*
1975 *Missale Romanum*	1985 *Sacramentary*
2000 *Missale Romanum*	2010 *Roman Missal*

Why is the English translation of the 2000 *Missale Romanum* significantly different from translations of the 1970 and 1975 typical editions?

The English translation of the 2000 *Missale Romanum* is significantly different from the translations of the 1970 and 1975 typical editions because of the different methods of translation used. When the 1970 and 1975 editions were translated, ICEL was guided by a method called "dynamic equivalence" (cf. *Comme le prévoit*). The translation of the 2000 edition was done using the method of "formal correspondence" (cf. *Liturgiam authenticam*).

How does "dynamic equivalence" differ from "formal correspondence"?

"Dynamic equivalence" is usually explained as "meaning-for-meaning" translation. It tries to look for the equivalent in meaning of the words from the original (Latin) to the receptor language (English). To effectively and faithfully communicate the message of the original text, it does not strictly follow the exact wording or word-order of the Latin original. Thus, it makes some adaptations in the process. It may be more suited for proclamation, but "something" in the original is lost when translated in the vernacular.

On the other hand, "formal correspondence" is usually described as "word-for-word" translation. It has the tendency to use the same wording and word-order of the original text. To avoid misinterpretation, it tries to preserve the Latin words. It may seem accurate by being literal, but it often requires explanations.

The translation of the three typical editions of *The Roman Missal* may be likened to a pendulum. "Dynamic equivalence" has swung the translation process to the receptor language (English) because it is more concerned with the understandability in the vernacular. "Formal correspondence" swings it back to the original text (Latin) because it places more importance on the qualities of the source language.

Moreover, it will be helpful to mention here that these two methods of translation are also used in translating the Bible. For example, the *New American Bible* used "formal correspondence." The *Good News Bible* was guided by "dynamic equivalence."

To illustrate, let us look at the English translation of the Latin *Et cum spiritu tuo (And with your spirit / And also with you).* We will have a more detailed discussion of this familiar reply in the next chapter. Here, we only wish to illustrate the difference between the two methods of translation. At the same time, we also wish to point out that the 1973 translation is also biblical! One biblical reference of the famous response is *Galatians* 6:18. The *New American Bible* reads: "The grace of our Lord Jesus Christ **be with your spirit**, brothers. Amen." The *Good News Bible*: "May the grace of our Lord Jesus Christ **be with you all**, my friends. Amen" (Emphases added).

What is the most significant character of the new translation?

The third typical edition of *The Roman Missal* is marked by faithful correspondence in verbal and grammatical structure of the Latin original text. The carefully chosen words express the theological accuracy, biblical connections, and dignified rhythm of the Roman Rite. As beautifully put in the website for *The Roman Missal* posted by the U.S. Bishops Committee on Divine Worship: "**New Words: A Deeper Meaning, but the Same Mass**" *(http://www. usccb.org/romanmissal/).*

Chapter II

"NEW WORDS: A DEEPER MEANING"

In order to further appreciate why the new English translation of *The Roman Missal* emphasizes the use of formal, transcendent language in the celebration of the Holy Mass, we may use the celebration of Memorial Day in the United States as our springboard since the Holy Mass is also a Memorial celebration.

In the U.S., Memorial Day is celebrated *formally* and informally on the last Monday in May every year. One example of its *formal* celebration is the event that takes place in Arlington National Cemetery in which the President of the United States is present. Here, dignitaries wear their formal attire and the soldiers in their military garb. After the wreath laying and observance of silence, the U.S. President delivers in solemn words his inspiring speech remembering the men and women who offered their lives for their nation and its values. Then, he salutes America's fighting forces, both living and dead.

In contrast, many people informally observe Memorial Day by visiting cemeteries, joining in the parades, or watching concerts wearing their casual attire. Their language is obviously conversational.

The Holy Mass is the *formal* celebration of the Memorial of Christ's passion, death, and resurrection. The fact that the Priest and the ministers wear sacred vestments (cf. *GIRM* 120) points to its formal, sacred character. As Pope Francis reminds us, "Vatican Council II calls it the 'sacred action par excellence,' adding that 'no other action of the Church can equal its efficacy by the same title and to the same degree' ("Sacrosanctum Concilium," 7)" (Pope Francis' Message to the German National Eucharistic Congress, June 9, 2013: http://www.zenit. org/en/articles/pope-francis-message-to-the-german-national-eucharistic-congress).

> **The Holy Mass is the *formal* celebration of the Memorial of Christ's passion, death, and resurrection.**

Dressed in formal clothes, we come together, not as spectators like those people watching concerts on Memorial Day, but as active participants like the soldiers who salute the President as he passes in front of them. Just as the soldiers are respectful in their language because of the presence of U.S. dignitaries, we also use formal, sacred language because of the presence of the Most High God. We use words that remind us of the marvelous deeds of God and the life-giving Sacrifice of Christ.

As we leave our private homes and "go to the house of the Lord" (*Ps* 122:1), we also leave behind the noises of the world so that we may enter into the mystery of God's presence, properly listen to his word, and worthily celebrate the Eucharist. For this reason, it is recommended that, before Holy Mass begins, **sacred silence** "be observed in the church, in the sacristy, in the vesting room, and in adjacent areas" (*GIRM* 45). Thus, we turn off or put into silent mode our cell phones and iPods. During this silence, we may quietly pray the prayers before Mass provided in Appendix A on pages 121-124. Each of us may also think of our own intentions, the personal problems and burdens we carry, including our joys and hopes, which will be offered in the prayers especially in the offering of Christ's Body and Blood.

While our spiritual preparation for the celebration of the Holy Mass is initially private and personal, the fact that we come together in the church signifies that the event to take place is not a private celebration but a communal one. We are gathered together as one Body of Christ and each one of us is an important part of it. In his famous pastoral letter *Gather Faithfully Together*, Cardinal Roger Mahony, Archbishop Emeritus of Los Angeles, quotes from an instruction written by a third century bishop:

> Exhort the people to be faithful to the assembly of the Church. Let them not fail to attend, but let them gather faithfully

> together. Let no one deprive the Church
> by staying away; if they do, they deprive
> the Body of Christ of one of its members!
> (*Didascalia*, chapter 13) (Mahony, 1997, 2).

Each one of us is an important part of the gathered Body of Christ. What would you feel if in your family gathering a brother or sister of yours is missing? The same feeling is felt by Christ when one of us is absent in our Sunday assembly.

By coming together, we are responding to Christ's invitation: "Come to me, all you who labor and are burdened, and I will give you rest" (*Mt* 11:28). After a stressful week, Christ invites us individually and all who say "yes" become a Church community in the Holy Trinity.

We preeminently express our being "Church" when we come together and celebrate the Memorial of Christ's death and resurrection especially on Sunday, the day of the Lord, the day of the Church, and the day of rest. "For where two or three are gathered together in my name, there am I in the midst of them" (*Mt* 18:20). We are initially formed into one Eucharistic assembly by the Introductory Rites.

A. The Introductory Rites

The Introductory Rites consist of the Entrance, the Greeting, the Penitential Act, the *Kyrie*, the *Gloria*, and Collect. These rites begin our celebration, introduce us to the mystery, and prepare us as one community for the proper listening to God's word and worthy celebration of the Eucharist (cf. *GIRM* 46). Thus, they serve as key to all that follows and set the tone for the whole celebration.

The first major change in the part of the people introduced into the Introductory Rites is in the Greeting.

Greeting

We now say "And with your spirit" instead of the usual "And also with you" in response to any of the three introductory greetings that the Priest may choose. The most traditional formula used in the liturgy is the third greeting: "The Lord be with you."

"The Lord be with you."

"The Lord be with you" (*Dominus vobiscum*) remains unchanged in the new translation of *The Roman Missal*. This usual greeting goes back to the Hebrew Old Testament and the Christian New Testament. In the Book of *Ruth*, Boaz greets his harvesters, "The Lord be with you!" (2:4). In the gospel according to *Luke*, Archangel Gabriel greets Mary at the Annunciation: "Hail, favored one! The Lord is with you" (1:28).

It is interesting to note that the "**you**" in the English translation "The Lord be with **you**" (Emphasis added) could be singular or plural depending on how many persons are addressed by the greeting. But the original Latin formulation *Dominus vobiscum* is in the plural form. This is reflected in the Spanish translation: *El Señor esté con **vosotros*** (Emphasis added). This clearly shows that the Eucharistic Liturgy is indeed a ***public*** and not a private celebration. Thus, the opening sentence of the rubrics of the Introductory Rites begins with the words: "When the people are gathered, the Priest approaches the altar with the ministers while the Entrance Chant is sung" ("The Order of Mass," *The Roman Missal* 1).

Because the greeting is Old Testament in origin, *Dominus* ("the Lord") merely referred to the indeterminate "God". But since its adoption by the Church, "the Lord" has been implicitly understood as referring to Jesus Christ, the Risen Lord, the Emmanuel ("God with us") who promised that "I am with you always, until the end of the age" (*Mt* 28:20). By this greeting, the Priest exercises his ministerial priesthood as our leader in the Eucharistic assembly. He "signifies the presence of the Lord to the community gathered there by means of the Greeting" (*GIRM* 50).

"And with your spirit."

The reply *Et cum spiritu tuo* (***And with your spirit***) is found in some letters of Saint Paul (cf. 2 *Tim* 4:22; *Phlm* 25; *Gal* 6:18; *Phil* 4:23). According to Father Joseph Jungmann, a Jesuit liturgical historian, *spiritus* *tuus*, from its Jewish origin, actually mean "your person" or simply "you." Thus, *Et cum spiritu tuo* really means "And with you too" (Jungmann, 1986, I:363). Using dynamic equivalence, the first ICEL translators of the 1970 and 1975 Latin typical editions of the *Missale Romanum* rendered it as "And also with you."

Now that *The Roman Missal* prefers the literal translation "And with your spirit", the next question is, what is the meaning of the word "spirit" in this reply of the people?

Father Anscar J. Chupungco, O.S.B., former president of the Pontifical Liturgical Institute in Rome and consultor to the Sacred Congregation of Divine Worship and the Sacraments, is a proponent of the view that the word "spirit" in our reply to the Priest's greeting cannot refer to the Holy Spirit received at priestly ordination. He explains that in Greek thought "spirit" (*pneuma*) "represents what is best and noblest in a person" (Chupungco, 2011, 18). He further cites an ancient Holy Saturday homily in which Christ searches for Adam among the dead. In reply to Adam's greeting, Christ says, "And with your spirit." Father Chupungo rightly observes that "we cannot interpret Christ's reply as affirmation that Adam possessed priestly spirit" (Chupungco, 2011, 19).

Father Robert L. Tuzik, who holds a PhD in liturgical studies from the University of Notre Dame, adds that when Saint Paul uses the word "spirit" (*pneuma*) he refers "to the spiritual part of man that is closest to or most like God. Our spirit is the immediate object of divine influence as well as the place where God dwells" (Tuzik, 2011, 48). For this reason, Father Paul Turner, former President of the North American Academy of Liturgy and currently serves as an ICEL facilitator, says, "The idea that it refers to the Holy Spirit of the ordained surely would have surprised Saint Paul, who prayed that the Lord Jesus would be with the 'spirit' of all the faithful" (Turner, 2011, 7).

However, some experts interpret "spirit" as referring to the gift of the Holy Spirit received by Priests at their ordination. Their basic argument is that the Priest could preside at the celebration of the Holy Mass not by his own power but by the power of the Holy Spirit that he received at his priestly ordination (cf. Magee, 2002, 152-171). They base their claim mostly on the Fathers of the Eastern Church, particularly Saint John Chrysostom (c. 347-407) and an Eastern theologian, Narsai of Nisibis (c. 399-502). Saint John Chrysostom says that by the words "And with your spirit" we are reminded

> that the right offering of the gifts is not a work of human nature, but that the mystic sacrifice is brought about by the grace of the Holy Spirit and His hovering over all. For he who is there is a man, but it is God who acts through him. Do not attend to the nature of the one you see, but understand the grace which is invisible (*PG* 50, 458).

Actually, both interpretations are complementary. The reply of Christ to Adam is to be interpreted according to the original Jewish meaning of *spiritus tuus* and the Greek *pneuma*, which is an acknowledgement of the fullness of the person who offers the greeting. Interpreting "spirit" as the gift of the Holy Spirit received by the Priest at his ordination may be considered as a development in the theological reflection of some Fathers of the Church. Perhaps their interpretation might be the basis why only the ordained ministers (Bishops, Priests, and Deacons) say the greeting, "The Lord be with you", and receive the reply, "And with your spirit".

This theological development is similar to the development of the interpretation of the word *missa*, "Mass". It comes from *Ite, missa est*, which originally means "dismissal" ("Go, the meeting is adjourned"). The Church adopted the secular expression and applied it to the solemn leave-taking in Church services. But gradually the meaning has evolved from "dismissal" to "mission". Pope Benedict XVI himself notes this development: "In antiquity, *missa* simply meant 'dismissal.' However in Christian usage it gradually took on a deeper meaning. The word 'dismissal' has come to imply a 'mission'" (*SacCar* 51). The Christian Eucharist has been called *"Holy Mass (Missa)*, because the liturgy in which the mystery of salvation is accomplished concludes with the sending forth (*missio*) of the faithful, so that they may fulfill God's will in their daily lives" (*CCC* 1332).

The view that refers "spirit" to the grace of the Holy Spirit received at priestly ordination seems to be the thinking of those responsible for the new English translation of the *Missale Romanum*. This is evident in the official website for *The Roman Missal* posted by the U.S. Bishops Committee on Divine Worship:

> The expression *et cum spiritu tuo* is only addressed to an ordained minister. Some scholars have suggested that *spiritu* refers to the gift of the spirit he received at ordination. In their response, the people assure the priest of the same divine assistance of God's spirit and, more specifically, help for the priest to use the charismatic gifts given to him in ordination and in so doing to fulfill his prophetic function in the Church. (http://old.usccb.org/romanmissal/translating_notes.shtml).

By replying "And with your spirit," we "return the greeting and express the prayerful wish that the priest will also be filled with the presence of the risen Lord, and that his ministry may receive the power and blessing of the Holy Spirit" (Chupungco, 2011, 21). "The usage of the word 'spirit' connects the greeting to its biblical roots, its historical usage, and the spiritual nature of the events about to take place" (Turner, 2011, 7).

But why is the dialogue repeated several times in the course of the liturgical celebration? The reciprocal greeting between the Priest and the people appears at the beginning of the key moments of the Eucharistic celebration to arouse the attention of the people and to intensify the presence of the Lord (Jungmann, 1986, I:362-363). The dialogue seems to colloquially announce: "Brothers and sisters, we are now gathered to pray. We are now to listen to Christ's Good News. We are now to thank the Lord. We are now to go and practice our faith."

When the Priest and the people greet one another, they remind each other that the Spirit of the Lord is present in their gathering forming them into Christ's Body, the Church. It is not a greeting that is abstract and impersonal such as the greeting popularized by the *Star Wars* films created by George Lucas: "May the Force be with you." Our God is a personal God who sent his Son into the world, who became fully human in the person of Jesus Christ assuring us of his abiding presence, "I am with you always" (*Mt* 28:20).

As Pope Francis says,

> God is not something vague, our God is not a God "spray", he is tangible; he is not abstract but has a name: "God is love". His is not a sentimental, emotional kind of love but the love of the Father who is the origin of all life, the love of the Son who dies on the Cross and is raised, the love of the Spirit who renews human beings and the world (Angelus Message, May 26, 2013: http://www.vatican.va/holy_father/ francesco/angelus/2013/documents/ papa-francesco_angelus_20130526_ en.html).

The General Instruction of the Roman Missal clearly explains the meaning of the exchange of greeting in the liturgy: "By this Greeting and the people's response, the mystery of the Church gathered together is made manifest" (*GIRM* 50). This is what is signified by the reciprocal salutation which is more than saying the conversational "Good morning."

> **"By this Greeting and the people's response, the mystery of the Church gathered together is made manifest"** (*GIRM* 50).

The Act of Penitence

Jesus says that before we offer our sacrifice, we must first be reconciled with our brothers and sisters (cf. *Mt* 5:23-25). It seems that the early Christians already observed this command as evidenced by the ancient document *Didache* which states, "On the Lord's own day, assemble in common to break bread and offer thanks; but first confess your sins" (*Didache* 14:1; cf. Johnson, 2006, 13). This confession of sins is given emphasis in the new translation.

"Greatly sinned."

The new translation "I have **greatly** sinned" appears as inaccurate translation of the Latin *peccavi nimis* which literally means "I have sinned exceedingly" or "I have sinned too much". Experts say that *nimis* is translated as "greatly" because it biblically echoes the words of the repentant King David, "I have sinned greatly in doing this thing" (*1 Chr* 21:8; cf. *2 Sam* 24:10).

What was "this thing" that King David did that offended God? He took a census of Israel. But was taking census *per se* sinful? Of course not. Census then was taken for conscription and taxation. Coming from his impressive military victories against the Ammonites, Syrians, and Philistines (cf. *1 Chr* 18-20), King David committed the sin of pride! He did the census to know the strength of his nation, to raise more money for his military, and thus to glorify himself. Instead of trusting God in winning his battles, he counted on the number and strength of his soldiers.

The lust of the flesh had led King David to commit the sin of adultery with Bathsheba and the sin of murder of her husband Uriah (cf. *2 Sam* 11). Now the lust for power and self-exaltation led him to the sin of pride. In both of these great sins, King David confessed and repented. He owned that he had "greatly sinned".

Our time is no different from King David's. With lust for military, political, and economic powers of rich countries, poor nations are bullied and taken advantage of. And with a lot of flesh in the Internet, movies, and magazines, the sins of adultery and murder are in the daily news. In our personal lives, when we become successful in our career or business, we tend to forget God. Like King David, we cease to trust God in our victories and we count on our newfound wealth and power.

In the Holy Mass, we humble ourselves before the Lord and confess our sins of commission ("in what I have done") and omission ("and in what I have failed to do"). Like King David who constantly repented for his sins of lust and pride, we always do the Act of Penitence in every Mass we participate in to remind us that turning away from our sins is a lifelong process.

King David's repentance is a model of the conversion process (cf. *2 Sam* 12) which consists of *conflict, encounter, self-discovery*, and *transformation*. His conversion begins with the *conflict* between his covenant with God and his grave sins of adultery and pride. It is his *encounter* with the prophet Nathan (cf. *2 Sam* 12:1) and the prophet Gad (cf. *1 Chr* 21:11) that brings about his *self-discovery* ("I have sinned greatly in doing this thing") and that leads to his *transformation* by experiencing God's loving forgiveness.

"Through my fault, through my fault, through my most grievous fault."

Here, the Latin *mea culpa, mea culpa, mea maxima culpa* is now translated as "**through my fault, through my fault, through my most grievous fault**". The 1973 translation omitted the two phrases *mea culpa, mea maxima culpa.* It is precisely from this part of the *Confiteor* ("I confess") that the expression *mea culpa* in popular usage has been derived. *Mea culpa* is an admission of having made a mistake. The restoration of the triple "my fault" is not only an accurate translation, but the repetition of the words also makes us truly humble before the great God and deepens our feeling of unworthiness.

Although there is no sacramental absolution of our sins at this general confession (cf. *GIRM* 51), we must note the healing power of the Holy Mass. Since ancient times, the Eucharist has been called "the medicine of immortality." It has the power to heal our minor sins reconciling us with God and with our brothers and sisters.

But if we have committed grave sins, we are to go first to the Sacrament of Reconciliation or Confession. As then Cardinal Ratzinger, now Pope Benedict XVI, clarified:

> The Eucharist is not itself the sacrament of reconciliation, but in fact it presupposes that sacrament. It is the *sacrament of the reconciled*, to which the Lord invites all those who have become one with him; who certainly still remain weak sinners, but yet have given their hand to him and have become part of his family (Ratzinger, 2003, 60).

The words "through my fault, through my fault, through my most grievous fault" are accompanied by the action of "striking their breast". This is a practice that is restored by the new translation. It is done by tapping the chest with a clenched fist. It is a symbolic way of recalling the action of the repentant tax collector who "beat his breast and prayed, 'O God, be merciful to me a sinner'" (*Lk* 18:13). Like the tax collector, we must continually "beat" our breast symbolizing our continuous need for God's mercy and forgiveness.

The Gloria

After we are assured of God's loving mercy and forgiveness, we are inspired to sing praise to God. Being a joyful hymn, the *Gloria* is sung or recited on festive occasions: Sundays (except during Advent and Lent), solemnities and feasts, and "special celebrations of a more solemn character" (*GIRM* 53). It is called the "Angelic Hymn" because it begins with the words of the angels when the birth of Christ the Lord was announced to the shepherds: "Glory to God in the highest and on earth peace to those on whom his favor rests" (*Lk* 2:14). The birth of the Messiah has brought two-fold effect: the glory of God and peace to man.

The glory of God is manifested in his creation which reaches its peak when the Son of God, Jesus Christ, became a human being and "was born of the Virgin Mary" affirming that we are indeed created in God's image and likeness.

> God created mankind in his image;
> in the image of God he created them;
> male and female he created them (*Gen* 1:27).

This image of God in us has been distorted by sin which has made us enemies of God (cf. *Rom* 5:10). When the Word of God became one of us, suffered, died, and rose again, he restored the divine image in us and became the perfect man.

> He is the image of the invisible God,
> the firstborn of all creation (*Col* 1:15).

Before Christ came, we were at war with God, with ourselves, with others, and creation. When God became man in the person of Jesus Christ, we could now begin to be at peace with our Creator, with our conscience, with our neighbors, and with our environment.

> And the Word became flesh
> and made his dwelling among us,
> and we saw his glory, the glory
> as of the Father's only Son,
> full of grace and truth (*Jn* 1:14).

This is why his birth was revealed by the angels in the highest heavens and in the most exalted degrees.

"And on earth peace to people of good will."

The Latin *et in terra pax hominibus bonae voluntatis* was rendered by the 1973 translation simply as "and peace to his people on earth". The new translation literally translated the Latin text as "**and on earth peace to people of good will**." Experts say that the "good will" referred to in the new translation is not people's good will as the text seems to imply but God's goodwill, the favor and grace given to those whom he has chosen. This is clearly indicated in *Lk* 2:14 in the following modern versions of the Bible: "and on earth peace to those on whom his favor rests" (*New American Bible*), "and on earth peace for those he favours" (*New Jerusalem Bible*), "and peace on earth to those with whom he is pleased!" (*Good News Bible*).

If peace is limited to only those whom God has favored, does this mean that God has favorites? Isn't it that the peace and reconciliation brought forth by Christ is for all? Indeed, God loves each one of us whom he has created according to his image and likeness. "For God so loved the world that he gave his only Son, so that everyone who believes in him might not perish but might have eternal life" (*Jn* 3:16). Yes, we have all been favored by God through his Son, Jesus Christ. But each of us has to freely accept this gratuitous offer of God. Our wills are to conform to God's goodwill. It is only those who will generously respond to his holy will that will have that "peace" and will be counted among "his people on earth."

"We praise you, we bless you, we adore you, we glorify you, we give you thanks for your great glory."

The list of Latin praises *Laudamus te, benedicimus te, adoramus te, glorificamus te, gratias agimus tibi propter magnam gloriam tuam* is faithfully echoed in the new translation: "**We praise you, we bless you, we adore you, we glorify you, we give you thanks for your great glory**." Happily, the new Roman Missal has restored the five laudatory verbs: praise, bless, adore, glorify, and give thanks, which the 1973 translation simplified and reduced into three ("we worship you, we give you thanks, we praise you for your glory").

Father Joseph Jungmann said, "the accent is not on the precise and distinctive meaning of each word but on the common basic concept of acclaiming and extolling the greatness of God" (Jungmann, I:352).

However, the expression "**we bless you**" seems strange to ordinary Catholics. Because many Catholics have been used to blessings of persons, places, and things, we seem to have limited the meaning of the word "bless" to the divine favor and protection we request of God: "Bless us, O Lord, . . .", "Bless this food . . .", "Bless this house . . ." We joyfully sing "God Bless America". We even say, "God bless you", after a sneeze. We also associate blessing with the Sign of the Cross. With this understanding, it seems surprising to ordinary Catholics to say to God: "we bless you"!

So, what do we mean when we say or sing to God in the *Gloria*, "we bless you"?

When we bless God, we praise him, worship him, and thank him for his goodness and greatness. This understanding of "bless" is primarily expressed in the Old Testament. "But when you have eaten and are satisfied, you must *bless* the LORD, your God, for the good land he has given you" (*Dt* 8:10). "I will *bless* the LORD at all times; his praise shall be always in my mouth" (*Ps* 34:2). "Sing to the LORD, *bless* his name; proclaim his salvation day after day (*Ps* 96:2). "All your works give you thanks, LORD, and your faithful *bless* you" (*Ps* 145:10) (Emphases added).

In this context, "to bless" in the Old Testament does not mean "to make the Sign of the Cross" (!). In Hebrew "to bless" is "to kneel" (*barakh*). "To kneel" before God is "to praise" him. Closely related to the Hebrew word *barakh* is *berakah* meaning "a blessing". The Greek Septuagint (LXX) used *eulogein* ("to speak well"; "to praise", "to bless"), from which we derive the word "eulogy", a speech in praise especially of a deceased person. The Latin Vulgate rendered it as *benedicere* (*bene* = well; *dicere* = "to speak"; hence, "to speak well of" or "to bless"). In Spanish, we say *bendecir* which has the same literal meaning as in Greek and Latin, "to speak well" ("to bless", "to praise").

So, when we read from the gospel that Jesus embraced the children "and blessed them, placing his hands on them" (*Mk* 10:16), we should not imagine that Jesus made a Sign of the Cross over the children. Remember that at the time of Jesus and even after his death, cross was a sign of scandal. The cross was their "electric chair" for criminals. What a cruel and brutal way to die! Thus, Saint Paul proclaimed that "Christ crucified" was "a stumbling block to Jews and foolishness to Gentiles" (*1 Cor* 1:23). When the Bible says that Jesus "blessed" the children, it means that Jesus prayed over them. He said a prayer of blessing over the children, he spoke well of them, and he said good words about them.

This is also how we should "bless" our children and the people we admire. When we praise them, we speak well of them. We say good words about them. We appreciate their good qualities. This will surely build them up as children of God.

In blessing or praising the Most High God, we are also "to speak well of" him by using "good words". As Blessed John Paul II said, when we are assembled to pray together as a Church especially at Holy Mass, we must use "*a language of praise and worship which fosters respect and gratitude for God's greatness, compassion and power . . .*", a language that fosters "the dignity and beauty of the celebration itself, while faithfully expressing the Church's faith and unity" (cf. *Ad limina*, 1993, 2).

> **At Holy Mass, we must use *"a language of praise and worship which fosters respect and gratitude for God's greatness, compassion and power . . .",* a language that fosters "the dignity and beauty of the celebration itself, while faithfully expressing the Church's faith and unity"** (Blessed John Paul II, *Ad limina*, 1993, 2).

Restoring the five ways of extolling the glory of God does not only express faithfulness to the Latin text, but also it is one instance that signifies the overarching concern of reforming the liturgy reformed by Vatican II ("reform of the reform"): to emphasize the sacred, spiritual character of the liturgy. It redirects our attention to God. The primary purpose of the Eucharistic assembly is to adore God and not to socialize. Worship is God-centered (theocentric), not human-centered (anthropocentric).

As Pope Francis reminds us, "Worshipping the Lord means that we are convinced before him that he is the only God, the God of our lives, the God of our history." The Pope continues:

> This has a consequence in our lives: we have to empty ourselves of the many small or great idols that we have and in which we take refuge, on which we often seek to base our security. They are idols that we sometimes keep well

hidden; they can be ambition, a taste for success, placing ourselves at the centre, the tendency to dominate others, the claim to be the sole masters of our lives, some sins to which we are bound, and many others. . . . Worshipping is stripping ourselves of our idols, even the most hidden ones, and choosing the Lord as the centre, as the highway of our lives. . . . The Lord is the only God of our lives, and he invites us to strip ourselves of our many idols and to worship him alone (http://www.vatican.va/holy_father/ francesco/homilies/2013/documents/ papa-francesco_20130414_omelia- basilica-san-paolo_en.html).

With too much focus on oneself and social networking today, it seems that the Mass is reduced to a fellowship gathering of acquaintances and friends. The commentary of Father Joseph Jungmann in 1948 on the *Gloria* particularly on the five successive words of acclaiming God remains true and valid today. He said:

We direct our glance wholly to God's glory, God's grandeur. We are happy to be allowed to praise His glory. For that reason a song such as this has such wonderful power to free men from any egoistic narrowness and to bring them all together on a higher plane (Jungmann, I:352).

Immediately after addressing the "Lord God, heavenly King, O God, almighty Father," the new translation of the *Gloria* transitions to address the "Lord Jesus Christ, Only Begotten Son, Lord God, Lamb of God, Son of the Father". Why does the song shift gear from the Father to his Son Jesus Christ?

"Our grateful glance toward God's glory moves naturally on toward Christ, in whom that glory was revealed to us" (Jungmann, I:353). At the Last Supper, Jesus prayed: "Father, the hour has come. Give glory to your son, so that your son may glorify you . . . I glorified you on earth by accomplishing the work that you gave me to do. Now glorify me, Father, with you, with the glory that I had with you before the world began. I revealed your name to those whom you gave me out of the world" (*Jn* 17:1-6).

Thus, we do not only "bless" the Father, but we also "bless" the Son. When we meditate on the Stations of the Cross, we pray before each station:

> We adore you, O Christ, and **we bless you**,
> because by your holy cross,
> you have redeemed the world (Emphasis added).

"Only Begotten Son."

The new translation has literally rendered the Latin *Fili Unigenite* as "**Only Begotten Son**". The 1973 translation omitted the word "Begotten" perhaps because modern versions of the Bible render it simply as "only Son". The *New American Bible* reads: "For God so loved the world that he gave his only Son" (*Jn* 3:16). The *Good News Bible*: "For God loved the world so much that he gave his only Son" (*Jn* 3:16). But the first Catholic English Bible, the *Douay-Rheims Bible,* includes the word "begotten": "For God so loved the world, as to give his only begotten Son" (*Jn* 3:16). The Latin *Unigenitus* is a compound word of *uni* (only) and *genitus* (begotten). The Greek origin is *Monogenes* which is also a compound word consisting of *mono* (only*)* and *genes* (begotten*).*

Is there any doctrinal content in the phrase "Only Begotten Son"? Jeremy Driscoll, OSB, professor of Monastic Studies and Liturgy at Mt. Angel Abbey, Oregon, and at San Anselmo, Rome, states, "One of the clearest examples of the doctrinal dimensions of the use of '*Unigenitus*' is found in the Opening Prayer on Monday in the weekdays of the Season of Christmas before the Epiphany of the Lord" (Driscoll in *The Voice of the Church*, 2001, 77). Below we will use the Collect of the third typical edition of *The Roman Missal* in reference to the relevant phrase cited by Driscoll:

> . . . that your Only Begotten Son
> is with you for ever in your glory
> and was born of the Virgin Mary
> in a body truly like our own . . .
> (Collect, Monday, Weekdays of Christmas Time)

Here the contrast between *Unigenitus* ("Only Begotten Son") and *natum de Maria Virgine* ("born of the Virgin Mary") is clearly brought out. Christ is "born of the Father before all ages" (Nicene Creed) and Jesus "was born of the Virgin Mary" in time.

"Only Begotten Son" is one of the ancient titles of Christ. The Church in the fourth century was threatened by the Arian heresy that denied Christ's divinity. The Church fathers of that period especially Saint Athanasius stressed that the Bible speaks of a "begetting" of the Son, not a creation. C.S. Lewis says, "To beget is to become the father of: to create is to make" (Lewis, 1987, 242). What's the difference? C.S. Lewis continues:

> When you beget, you beget something of the same kind as yourself. A man begets human babies, a beaver begets little beavers and a bird begets eggs which turn into little birds. But when you make, you make something of a different kind from yourself. A bird makes a nest, a beaver builds a dam, a man makes a wireless set . . . (Lewis, 1987, 242).

"Begotten" is a biological metaphor to help us understand the unique filial relationship between God the Father and God the Son. "Only Begotten Son" means that Jesus Christ shares the *genus* of God the Father, that Jesus Christ is the true *genetic* Son, having the same divine *nature* or *essence* of the Father. Thus, the Nicene Creed states, "God from God, Light from Light, true God from true God, begotten, not made".

Through Jesus Christ, the "Only Begotten Son" of God the Father, we as believers become God's adopted sons and daughters. "In love he predestined us to be adopted as his sons through Jesus Christ, in accordance with his pleasure and will" (*Eph* 1:5). "But when the fullness of time had come, God sent his Son, born of a woman, born under the law, to ransom those under the law, so that we might receive adoption. As proof that you are children, God sent the spirit of his Son into our hearts, crying out, 'Abba, Father!' So you are no longer a slave but a child, and if a child then also an heir, through God" (*Gal* 5:4-7). "The Spirit heals and transforms those who receive him by conforming them to the Son of God. The fruit of the sacramental life is that the Spirit of adoption makes the faithful partakers in the divine nature by uniting them in a living union with the only Son, the Savior" (*CCC* 1129).

If the richest man in the world would invite you to a banquet with the promise that he would adopt you as his son or daughter and make you his heir, would you not come? In the Eucharistic banquet, Christ is inviting us to be united with him in the Spirit so that we may share in his divinity making us adopted sons and daughters and heirs of God the Father, Creator of heaven and earth!

We have been adopted sons and daughters of God the Father because Jesus Christ has taken away our sins. John the Baptist declares, "Behold, the Lamb of God, who takes away the sin of the world" (*Jn* 1:29).

"You take away the sins of the world."

The Latin clause *qui tollis peccata mundi* is rendered by the new translation as "you take away the **sins** of the world". The new translation has faithfully translated *peccata* as "sins". The 1973 translation used a singular form ("sin") perhaps because it wanted to faithfully echo the biblical *peccatum* (sin) of *Jn* 1:29. There is no theological or doctrinal problem whether it is "sin" or "sins" because our individual, personal sins are substantially contained in the collective sin of the world. In the Old Testament reference to the sacrificial lamb, sin is in the plural form. "But he was pierced for our offenses, crushed for our sins" (*Is* 53:5).

"Lamb of God" is another ancient title of Christ used by the early Church. The title recalls the Old Testament lamb provided by God to Abraham for sacrifice in place of his son Isaac (cf. *Gen* 22:8-13), the Passover lamb whose blood saved Israelites from death (cf. *Ex* 12:23), and the lamb from Isaiah whose sacrifice would redeem Israel (cf. *Is* 53:7). To us Christians, Jesus Christ is the true Paschal Lamb, who offers himself for our deliverance from darkness and death (cf. 1 *Pt* 1:18-19). He died on the cross not only for Israel but also for the "world" which includes you and me. Jesus Christ sets us free from sin and takes away our guilt. Since the title reminds us of God's great mercy, we say the supplication: "have mercy on us".

The Collect

The Collect is the "Opening Prayer" of the 1973 translation. The new Roman Missal prefers the literal translation of the Latin *Collecta*. It is called Collect because this prayer "collects" or "gathers together" the intentions we call to mind during the ***brief silence*** after the priest says the concise invitation: "Let us pray." At the end of this climactic prayer of the Introductory Rites, we all say the Hebrew "Amen" meaning that we make the prayer as our own, believing that God will make it happen.

Now that we have been gathered as a community, contritely confessed our sins, joyfully praised God's glory, and humbly lifted up our Mass intentions, we are ready to properly listen to God's word.

B. The Liturgy of the Word

The Liturgy of the Word consists of the First Reading, the Responsorial Psalm, the Second Reading, the Acclamation before the Gospel, the Gospel, the Homily, the Profession of Faith, and the Universal Prayer of the Faithful. In the biblical readings God speaks to us and "Christ, present in his word, proclaims the Gospel" (*GIRM* 29). We respond to the word of God after it has been explained in the Homily by means of the Profession of Faith. Inspired by the Divine Word, we pour out our "petitions by means of the Universal Prayer for the needs of the whole Church and for the salvation of the whole world" (*GIRM* 55).

The Biblical Readings

In his Apostolic Exhortation *Verbum Domini*, Pope Benedict XVI speaks of the way we ought to approach the word of God. Quoting Saint Jerome, the Pope says: "'When we approach the [Eucharistic] Mystery, if a crumb falls to the ground we are troubled. Yet when we are listening to the word of God . . . we pay no heed, what great peril should we not feel?'"

Like the Eucharistic food, the word of God also nourishes us. Jesus himself likens the word of God to food. He says, "One does not live by bread alone, but by every word that comes forth from the mouth of God" (*Mt* 4:4). Due reverence is given to the word of God by attentively listening to it.

To properly listen to the word of God, Pope Benedict XVI emphasizes the importance of silence.

> Ours is not an age which fosters recollection; at times one has the impression that people are afraid of detaching themselves, even for a moment, from the mass media. For this reason, it is necessary nowadays that the People of God be educated in the value of silence. Rediscovering the centrality of God's word in the life of the Church also means rediscovering a sense of recollection and

inner repose. The great patristic tradition teaches us that the mysteries of Christ all involve silence. Only in silence can the word of God find a home in us, as it did in Mary, woman of the word and, inseparably, woman of silence. Our liturgies must facilitate this attitude of authentic listening: *Verbo crescente, verba deficient* [When the Word appears, words fail]. (http://www.vatican.va/holy_father/benedict_xvi/apost_exhortations/documents/hf_ben-xvi_exh_20100930_verbum-domini_en.html).

If we need moments of silence when we digest inspiring quotations as "food for thought", we also ought to have periods of sacred silence in order that we can prayerfully meditate on the word of God. "The Liturgy of the Word is to be celebrated in such a way as to favor meditation" (*GIRM* 56). Thus, haste is to be avoided and silence is recommended "before the Liturgy of the Word itself begins, after the First and Second Reading, and lastly at the conclusion of the Homily" (*GIRM* 56).

The Gospel

"The reading of the Gospel constitutes the high point of the Liturgy of the Word" (*GIRM* 60). It is carried out with special rites, ministry, book, and acclamations. As a sign of reverence, we stand at the singing of the Alleluia or Verse before the Gospel as the Deacon or Priest processes to the ambo raising the *Book of the Gospels*, accompanied by two candle bearers and thurifer on festive occasions. He makes the Sign of the Cross on the book and on the forehead, lips, and breast. After we acclaim "Glory to you, O Lord", the Deacon or Priest incenses the book and at the end of the reading he acclaims "The Gospel of the Lord" (not simply "The word of the Lord" as in the first two readings) and he kisses the book.

The major change in the part of the people in this part of the celebration is the response to the greeting "The Lord be with you."

"And with your spirit."

This is the second time in the entire celebration of the Holy Mass that we give this reply, "And with your spirit." At this key moment of the Liturgy of the Word, our attention is again called to the presence of the Lord in the assembly as the Gospel is announced. Our reply to the ordained minister, "And with your spirit", acquires a deeper meaning because he will make present Christ's Good News to us today, here and now. The mystery of the presence of the Lord in the Church gathered together is made more manifest and intense because our hearts will be "burning" (*Lk* 24:32) within us as Jesus Christ proclaims his Gospel to us his Body, the Church, and nourishes us with his life-giving word.

After the Priest "breaks" God's word to us in the Homily, the major changes in the parts of the people in the Liturgy of the Word are mainly in the Nicene Creed and the Apostles' Creed.

The Nicene Creed

Containing the essential elements of our faith, the Creed is like a multi-vitamin of our Christian life in one capsule. Do you want to be healthy, happy, and holy? Take the enriched multi-vitamin of our Catholic faith not only once a week at Sunday Mass, but take it daily when praying the Rosary.

The Rosary is a plateful of prayer supplements to our Eucharistic food because it contains the rich mysteries of our faith. As we all know, it begins with our multi-vitamin which we also take every Sunday Mass. To appreciate its rich and vital contents, let us examine the new, enriching "ingredients" introduced by our Mother, the Church. Let us begin with the very first ingredient which happens to be the name of our multi-vitamin. The "Creed" derives its name from its first word in Latin: *Credo* ("I believe").

"I believe."

The change from "We believe" to "**I believe**" (*Credo*) in the new translation is not only being literal but it also emphasizes the personal faith we initially professed at our baptism. This is the "door of faith" referred to by Pope Benedict XVI when he announced the *Year of Faith.*

> The "door of faith" (*Acts* 14:27) is always open for us, ushering us into the life of communion with God and offering entry into his Church. It is possible to cross that threshold when the word of God is proclaimed and the heart allows itself to be shaped by transforming grace. To enter through that door is to set out on a journey that lasts a lifetime. It begins with baptism (cf. *Rom* 6:4) (*PF* 1).

At baptism, each of us publicly declares the common faith of the Church. "Whoever says 'I believe' says 'I pledge myself to what we believe'"

(*CCC* 185). The Creed, then, is our pledge of loyalty to God and the Church.

When we recite *together* our Pledge of Allegiance to the United States Flag, we use the first person singular "I" and not the plural "We". "**I** pledge allegiance to the flag of the United States of America, and to the republic for which it stands, one nation under God, indivisible, with liberty and justice for all" (Emphasis added).

Similarly, we recite *together* the Creed in the first person singular "I". We recited our first allegiance to God and the Church at our baptism when we first received the Creed from the Church. At the Holy Mass on Sundays, Solemnities, and "particular celebrations of a more solemn character" (*GIRM* 68), we renew our baptism by joyfully singing or reciting together with the Priest: "I believe".

Jesus says, "Believe in the gospel" (*Mk* 1:15). Faith is our response to the Good News which we first publicly profess at our baptism. The Bible calls this "the obedience of faith" (cf. *Rom* 1:5; 16:26). "To obey (from the Latin *ob-audire*, to 'hear or listen to') in faith is to submit freely to the word that has been heard, because its truth is guaranteed by God, who is Truth itself" (*CCC* 144).

Abraham and the Virgin Mary are great examples of the obedience of faith. "By faith Abraham obeyed when he was called to go out to a place that he was to receive as an inheritance; he went out, not knowing where he was to go" (*Heb* 11:8). "By faith Mary welcomes the tidings and promise brought by the angel Gabriel, believing that 'with God nothing will be impossible' and so giving her assent: 'Behold I am the handmaid of the Lord; let it be [done] to me according to your word'" (*CCC* 148).

Like Abraham and the Virgin Mary, we become obedient sons and daughters of God the Father and brethren of Jesus Christ when we listen to the word of God, internalize it, and translate it into action.

The Creed is also called "symbol of faith" just as a flag is a national symbol of a country.

> The Greek word *symbolon* meant half of a broken object, for example, a seal presented as a token of recognition. The broken parts were placed together to verify the bearer's identity. The symbol of faith, then, is a sign of recognition and communion between believers. *Symbolon* also means a gathering, collection, or summary. A symbol of faith is a summary of the principal truths of the faith and therefore serves as the first and fundamental point of reference for catechesis (*CCC* 188).

In the history of our Church, several creeds or symbols have been formulated, but two have gained wide and universal acceptance: the Apostles' Creed and the Nicene Creed.

> *The Apostles' Creed* is so called because it is rightly considered to be a faithful summary of the apostles' faith. It is the ancient baptismal symbol of the Church of Rome. Its great authority arises from this fact: it is

"the Creed of the Roman Church, the See of Peter, the first of the apostles, to which he brought the common faith" (*CCC* 194).

The Niceno-Constantinopolitan or Nicene Creed draws its great authority from the fact that it stems from the first two ecumenical Councils (in 325 and 381). It remains common to all the great Churches of both East and West to this day (*CCC* 195).

"Of all things visible and invisible."

The Latin phrase *visibilium omnium et invisibilium* is accurately translated as "**of all things visible and invisible**". The phrase finds echo in the ancient hymn of the early Church handed down to us by Saint Paul in his Letter to the *Colossians*:

> He is the image of the invisible God,
> the firstborn of all creation.
> For in him were created all things in heaven and on earth,
> the visible and the invisible,
> whether thrones or dominions or principalities or powers;
> all things were created through him and for him (*Col* 1:15-16).

The original Latin phrase wants to convey the objective and natural distinction between the material world and the spiritual world. The expression "visible and invisible" is descriptive of the **nature** of all things or beings that God has created. The 1973 rendition "seen and unseen" does not accurately express what the original Latin intends to impart. Angels are by nature "invisible" whether they stay in heaven or sent to earth. A human being is by nature "visible" although he may be "seen" or "unseen" depending upon the time and the person looking at him. A student physically present in a classroom is "visible" to his teacher and classmates but "unseen" by his mother cooking at home.

Furthermore, by stating that God is the maker "of all things visible and invisible", the Nicene Creed is making a clear statement to those who teach that only the spirit is good and the body is evil. Both visible (material) and invisible (spiritual) beings have been created by God the Father Almighty and both are good. "God looked at everything he had made, and found it very good" (*Gen* 1:31).

"Consubstantial."

Consistent with literal translation of the Latin text, *The Roman Missal* renders the Latin *consubstantialem* as **consubstantial**. The change from "one in Being" to "consubstantial" is indeed a major change in the wording of the Creed. But there is a good and valid reason for this change. The Creed is the Symbol and Profession of our Faith. If professional organizations like associations of doctors and lawyers use technical terms in their respective professions, the Church as an institution has also developed her own theological vocabulary to articulate her teachings and beliefs. As members of the Church, we need to understand the words that express our identity as being one Body of Christ. The Creed defines us Christian Catholics.

"Consubstantial" was a crucial theological term in the early Church. In the fourth century, the Church was forced to clarify one of the biblical titles of Christ, "Son of God" (*Jn* 1:49), because one of her children, Arius, taught that the relationship between Jesus Christ the Son and God the Father was just "Like Father, Like Son". Since the language of the Church then was Greek, Arius used the Greek word *homoiousios* ("like substance"). His teaching had caused so much confusion and division in the Church that it took a Council to decide on the christological issue: whether Jesus Christ was "like the substance" *(homoiousios)* of the Father or "of the same substance" (*homoousios*) as the Father. The issue was decided on a crucial single letter!

In 325 A.D., the Council of Nicea, the first Ecumenical Council of the Church, decided in favor of *homoousios*, "of the same substance", which, according to Pope Benedict XVI, is "the only philosophical term that was incorporated into the Creed. This philosophical term serves, however, to safeguard the reliability of the *biblical* term" (Ratzinger/Benedict XVI, 2007, 320).

When the Greek Nicene Creed was translated into Latin, *homoousion* was rendered as *consubstantialem* or "consubstantial" in English. It may be helpful to recall here another philosophical and theological term which is used to explain the mysterious change of the bread and wine into the Body and Blood of

Christ, "transubstantiation". Both "consubstantial" and "transubstantiation" have the same root word: "substance". Etymologically, it comes from the Latin preposition *sub* meaning "under" and the Latin present participle of the verb *stare* which is *stans* meaning "standing". Hence, "substance" literally means the thing "standing under", or the reality beneath the surface. Then Cardinal Ratzinger (now Pope Benedict XVI) referred to "substance" as "the profound and fundamental basis of being" (Ratzinger, 2003, 85).

In the philosophy of Aristotle, every material thing consists of two metaphysical principles: "substance" and "accidents". "Substance" is the essence of a thing and "accidents" are its physical properties. The term "accidents" comes from the Latin *accidens*, meaning "that which belongs to". For example, there are different types of bread (white bread, wheat bread, rye bread, matza, baguette, and bagel), but they have only one "substance" or "being" which is *bread*. Their shape, color, and weight are the "accidents". When a white sandwich bread is sliced, ripped into crumbs, mixed with milk, sugar, and eggs, and baked, it is changed into a pudding for dessert. Its former "substance" or "being" as sandwich bread is transformed into its present "substance" or "being" as pudding.

Speaking of transformation, we can mention here for further illustration the successful action film *Transformers.* In this American science fiction film, we see the alien robots transform themselves into beautiful cars and powerful trucks on Earth. Their "substance" or "being" as alien robots is changed into another "substance" or "being" as machineries on Earth.

The prefix *con* of the word "consubstantial" comes from the Latin preposition *cum* meaning "with". Hence, when we say "consubstantial" in the Creed, we mean that Christ is of the "same substance" (*homoousion*) *with* the Father. The former translation "one in Being" is not as accurate as "consubtantial" because "being" would include everything in a person or thing. "Substance" would refer more precisely to the "essence" of the person or thing. The former expression "one in Being with the Father" may be misinterpreted to mean that Jesus Christ is the same in everything with the Father. Jesus says, "The Father and I are one" (*Jn* 10:30). While God is One, the Three Divine Persons are distinct in their relationship. While we may use the analogy of 3 in 1 coffee to illustrate the Three Divine Persons in One God, such analogy is not only imperfect but it falls short of the unique personal relationship of the Divine Persons. The universal *Catechism of the Catholic Church* clarifies the technical use of the words "substance" and "person":

> The Church uses (I) the term "substance" (rendered also at times by "essence" or "nature") to designate the divine being in its unity, (II) the term "person" or "hypostasis" to designate the Father, Son and Holy Spirit in the real distinction among them, and (III) the term "relation" to designate the fact that their distinction lies in the relationship of each to the others (252).

> **"The Church uses the term 'substance' . . .
> to designate the divine being in its unity"**
> (*CCC* 252).

The Trinity is One. We do not confess three Gods, but one God in three persons, the "consubstantial Trinity". The divine persons do not share the one divinity among themselves but each of them is God whole and entire: "The Father is that which the Son is, the Son that which the Father is, the Father and the Son that which the Holy Spirit is, i.e. by nature one God." In the words of the Fourth Lateran Council (1215), "Each of the persons is that supreme reality, viz., the divine substance, essence or nature" (253).

The divine persons are really distinct from one another. "God is one but not solitary." "Father", "Son", "Holy Spirit" are not simply names designating modalities of the divine being, for they are really distinct from one another: "He is not the Father who is the Son, nor is the Son he who is the Father, nor is the Holy Spirit he who is the Father or the Son." They are distinct from one another in their relations of origin: "It is the Father who generates, the Son who is begotten, and the Holy Spirit who proceeds." The divine Unity is Triune (254).

Thus, Pope Benedict XVI says that the title of Christ as "Son of God" is "to be understood quite literally: Yes, in God himself there is an eternal dialogue between Father and Son, who are both truly one and the same God in the Holy Spirit" (Ratzinger/ Benedict XVI, 2007, 320).

To use an analogy, "Sodium chloride" is the scientific, chemical name for "common salt" or "table salt". The term "salt" is widely known and easily understood by ordinary people. But "sodium chloride" is used in the scientific world to identify the exact nature of this chemical compound.

Similarly, the simple descriptions of the relationship between God the Father and God the Son ("God from God, Light from Light, true God from true God, begotten, not made") seem to be understandable expressions. But a more accurate description of the unique relationship between the First Person and the Second Person of the Blessed Trinity has also been given a theological term: "consubstantial with the Father".

This life of the Blessed Trinity is the model of all human relationships especially of Christian families. Our universal catechism states:

> The Christian family is a communion of persons, a sign and image of the communion of the Father and the Son in the Holy Spirit. In the procreation and education of children it reflects the Father's work of creation. It is called to partake of the prayer and sacrifice of Christ. Daily prayer and the reading of the

> Word of God strengthen it in charity. The
> Christian family has an evangelizing and
> missionary task (*CCC* 2205).

Quoting Saint Augustine's *De Trinitate* (VIII, 8,
12: *CCL* 50, 287), Pope Benedict XVI says, "If you
see charity, you see the Trinity" (*Deus Caritas Est* 19).
Having been married for twenty years, I can say that I
have experienced the creative love of the *Father* when
I began to fall in love with my wife, Lucille. I was
able to compose beautiful love letters and poems. And
that creative love became procreative when we were
blessed with three lovely children: Maria, Topher, and
Angeline. The sufferings of married life have become
redemptive when we join our sacrifices with the
offering of the Body and Blood of Christ, the Only
Begotten *Son*, in the Holy Mass on Sundays. Thus,
the three rings of our marriage (engagement ring,
wedding ring, and suffering!) have been continuously
transformed by the *Holy Spirit* making us into ca-ring,
sha-ring, and perseve-ring Christian family.

"Incarnate."

The highly theological Latin formulation *Et
incarnatus est de Spiritu Sancto ex Maria Virgine,
et homo factus est* is now literally translated as "and
by the Holy Spirit **was incarnate** of the Virgin Mary,
and became man". The change from "**born** of the
Virgin Mary, and became man" to "**was incarnate** of
the Virgin Mary, and became man" is not only literal
but also doctrinal. The former formulation seems

to imply that Jesus Christ became man only after he had been born. Our faith teaches that Jesus Christ, the Divine Word, took the human condition not at his birth which we celebrate on Christmas (December 25) but at the Annunciation (March 25) when Mary said her "fiat" or "yes" to be the Mother of God. The universal catechism quotes Saint Irenaeus who said, "Christ became incarnate and was made man" (*CCC* 518). By the use of the theological term "incarnate", the new translation hopefully avoids the seeming misinterpretation which has a profound significance in the moral teaching of the Church especially with respect to the issues of abortion and respect for human life.

The Church has consistently taught that human life begins at conception. The right to life begins from womb to tomb. To force religious institutions, private health plans and employers to cover sterilization, contraception, and abortifacient drugs strikes at the very heart of the Christian faith on incarnation, not to mention the basic human right to follow one's conscience and the right to religious freedom.

To explain the meaning of the word "incarnate", an analogy from science again helps us understand the highly charged word. When water vapor turns into a liquid or ice phase, science calls it condensation. When God became human, the Church calls it *incarnation*. The word comes from the Latin verb *incarnare* which is a combination of the Latin preposition *in* (meaning "in" or "into") and the Latin noun *caro, carnis* (meaning "flesh"). Hence, literally, to be "incarnate" means "to be made flesh". In the

Bible, it is expressed as "And the Word became flesh" (*Jn* 1:14).

Mary's reply to angel Gabriel in the gospel of Luke, chapter 1, verse 38 ("Behold, I am the handmaid of the Lord. May it be done to me according to your word.") should also be our response to all the natural and human calamities that are thrown in our life. Mary's reply is a statement of humble submission to God's will and strong faith in God. We are called to repeat the same response when we feel God calls us to do what seems impossible. By saying our own *fiat* ("let it be done"), we are cooperating with God for his Word to take flesh or be incarnate in our life.

In the Holy Mass, we outwardly express our humble submission to God's will by making "a profound bow" at the words "and by the Holy Spirit was incarnate of the Virgin Mary, and became man", "but on the Solemnities of the Annunciation and of the Nativity of the Lord, all genuflect" (*GIRM* 137). As a corporate action, our ritual act of bowing our heads or bending our knees is our way of expressing that "we acknowledge the great *commercium*, the divine gift of the Son to humanity" (Foley, 2011, 193).

Apostles' Creed

In the United States and other English-speaking countries the Nicene Creed is the "default" (borrowing from computer language) and the Apostles' Creed is recommended "especially during Lent and Easter Time" ("The Order of Mass," *The Roman Missal* 19). The only major change in the Apostles' Creed is the expression "he descended into hell".

"He descended into hell."

The Latin formulation *descendit ad inferos* was rendered by the 1973 translation as "he descended to the dead." The new translation now is "he descended **into hell**". Did Jesus Christ really go to hell? Our English expressions that include the word "hell" such as "what the hell", "who the hell", "give someone hell", "for the hell of it", and "all hell broke loose" do not help us in understanding this article of the Apostles' Creed. This is so because the translation of the Latin *inferos* as "hell", as Father Chupungco observes, "does not correspond to the current understanding of hell" (Foley, 2011, 184). However, by literally translating the Latin *inferos* as "hell", the new translation exactly echoes the same words of the Apostles' Creed in the universal *Catechism of the Catholic Church* (See subtitle of *CCC* 631-637). For this reason, we need to clarify first the meaning of the word "hell".

In the Hebrew Old Testament, it was believed that when people died, whether good or bad, all descended to *Sheol* which is the common "place of the dead". *Sheol* was translated as *Hades* in the Greek Septuagint and as *Inferus* in the Latin Vulgate. Both the influential *King James Version* and the *Douay-Rheims Bible* literally translated *Inferus* as "hell". Biblically, "hell" as *Sheol, Hades,* or *Inferus* means the state or "the abode of the dead" (*CCC* 633).

Hence, when we profess in the Apostles' Creed "he descended into hell", we mean "that Jesus did really die" (*CCC* 636). As a human being, Jesus experienced real death. Indeed, he was "six feet under". Jesus himself had foretold in reference to the story of Jonah, "For as Jonah was three days and three nights in the belly of the whale, so will the Son of Man be three days and three nights in the heart of the earth" (*Mt* 12:40). This is the first meaning of "he descended into hell". But there is more to it than just Christ suffering death.

"He descended into hell" is an assertion that Christ triumphed over death releasing the good and holy men and women of the Old Testament. In the Letter to the Ephesians, it is said that Jesus Christ "descended into the lower [regions] of the earth" (*Eph* 4:9). He went to *Hades*. "I was dead, and behold, I am alive forevermore, and I have the keys of death and of Hades" (*Rev* 1:18). This abode of the dead, *Hades*, is the "hell" into which Christ descended. He did not go to *Gehenna*, "the unquenchable fire" (*Mk* 9:43-48) or "lake of fire" (*Rev* 20:14), which is generally the understanding today of the word "hell". Between decades of the Rosary, we ask Jesus to "save us from the fires of hell".

This picture of "hell" has been popularized in literature for example in Dante's *Inferno* in his *Divine Comedy*. And in the first English translations of the Bible especially the Protestant *King James Version* and the Catholic *Douay-Rheims Bible*, no distinction has been made between *Gehenna* and *Hades*. Both are translated as "hell". *Douay-Rheims Bible* reads: "And fear ye not them that kill the body, and are not able to kill the soul: but rather fear him that can destroy both soul and body in hell" (*Mt* 10:28). It is good that the *New American Bible* uses *Gehenna*: "And do not be afraid of those who kill the body but cannot kill the soul; rather, be afraid of the one who can destroy both soul and body in *Gehenna*" (*Mt* 10:28).

It is important to maintain the distinction between *Hades* and *Gehenna*. *Hades* is a temporary condition while *Gehenna* is eternal damnation. Christ descended into *Hades*, into the "Limbo of the Patriarchs" or "Limbo of the Fathers" or "bosom of Abraham" (*Lk* 16:22). In this light, we can understand why the patriarchs of the Old Testament were desiring for "a better homeland, a heavenly one" (*Heb* 11:16). "In his human soul united to his divine person" (*CCC* 637), Jesus "went to preach to the spirits in prison" (1 *Pet* 3:18-19). Their hope was fulfilled when Jesus Christ went to them and announced what he had promised to the good thief, "Today you will be with me in Paradise" (*Lk* 23:43). "Now since the children share in blood and flesh, he likewise shared in them, that through death he might destroy the one who has the power of death, that is, the devil, and free those who through fear of death had been subject to slavery all their life" (*Heb* 2:14-15). This scene of freeing the souls of the just is beautifully described in an ancient homily for Holy Saturday:

> Today a great silence reigns on earth, a great silence and a great stillness. A great silence because the King is asleep. The earth trembled and is still because God has fallen asleep in the flesh and he has raised up all who have slept ever since the world began . . . . He has gone to search for Adam, our first father, as for a lost sheep. Greatly desiring to visit those who live in darkness and in the shadow of death, he has gone to free from sorrow Adam in his bonds and Eve, captive with him—He who is both their God and the son of Eve . . . . "I am your God, who for your sake have become your son . . . . I order you, O sleeper, to awake. I did not create you to be a prisoner in hell. Rise from the dead, for I am the life of the dead." (PG 43, 440A, 452C; quoted in *CCC* 635).

When we profess "he descended into hell", we proclaim a very powerful and vivid description of God's unfathomable love. Death is supposed to be a "rest in peace". But Jesus Christ continued to work even in death. He searched for the just of the Old Testament so that they might receive their reward in heaven.

Today, Christ continues to descend into "hell" to save those who are already experiencing "hell" here on Earth. Christ continues to go down into our "hell" to pull us up from the pit of sin. When we separate ourselves from God, from nature, and from one another, Christ reaches down into our "hell". Our "hell" may be a mean officemate or unreasonable boss. It may be a lingering illness like cancer or diabetes. It may be the deep, painful sorrow for the death of a loved one. It may be the feeling of being desperate because we are deeply buried under a huge debt. It may be the feeling of being abandoned by a spouse.

If we continue to patiently hold on, if we continue to remain faithful like the just of the Old Testament, Christ will surely come "in his time" reaching out to us. This is the beauty of our Christian faith. We do not only see light at the end of the tunnel, but we also see our God entering into our tunnel!

Pope Benedict XVI assures us, "We believe with firm certitude that the Lord Jesus has conquered evil and death. With this sure confidence we entrust ourselves to him: he, present in our midst, overcomes the power of the evil one (cf. *Lk* 11:20)" (*PF* 15).

> **"We believe with firm certitude that the Lord Jesus has conquered evil and death"** (Benedict XVI).

After listening to God's word that is explained in the Homily and responding by saying the Profession of Faith and asking help for our needs, we are inspired to move our celebration from the ambo to the altar, from the table of the Word to the table of the Eucharist.

C. The Liturgy of the Eucharist

At the Last Supper, Jesus "took the bread, said the blessing, broke it, and gave it to them, saying, 'This is my body, which will be given for you; do this in memory of me.' And likewise the cup after they had eaten, saying, 'This cup is the new covenant in my blood, which will be shed for you'" (*Lk* 22:19-20). In faithful obedience to the command of Christ to "do this in memory of me", the Church has structured the Liturgy of the Eucharist according to what Christ said and did at the Last Supper:

- (1) The Preparation of the Gifts = Christ *taking* bread and wine
- (2) The Eucharistic Prayer = Christ *thanking* God the Father
- (3) The Communion Rite = Christ *breaking* the bread and *giving* his Body and Blood (cf. *GIRM* 72).

By the ritual actions of *taking* bread and wine, *thanking* God the Father for making the offerings the Body and Blood of Christ by sending the Holy Spirit, and *receiving* them to make us united to Christ, we join the Priest, "representing Christ the Lord" (*GIRM* 72), in making present in our banquet celebration the Paschal Sacrifice that Christ instituted at the Last Supper. Using computer language, by logging on with the "username" *takingthanking* and the "password" *breakinggiving,* we can access and participate in what happened at the Last Supper on Holy Thursday and the death of Christ on Good Friday and his resurrection on Easter Sunday.

The Preparation of the Gifts

As Jesus *took* bread and wine at the Last Supper, the Priest also *takes* bread and wine brought forward by the representatives of our community. As they are brought to the altar including other gifts like the money collected, we also offer ourselves that all our sacrifices may be united to the Sacrifice of Christ.

The only change in the part of the people at this juncture is the introduction of the word "**holy**" in reply to the invitation to pray that the *single* Sacrifice of Christ "may be acceptable to God, the almighty Father."

"Holy."

Our reply in the new translation includes the word "holy": "for our good and the good of all his **holy** Church" which is a faithful translation of the Latin *ad utilitatem quoque nostrum totiusque Ecclesiae suae **sanctae*** (Emphasis added). The introduction of the word "holy" is significant because it is in line with the general intention which is "to enhance the sacred meaning of the liturgical actions, objects, and personages" (Foley, 2007, 201).

Every celebration of the Holy Mass is the action of the whole Mystical Body of Christ, that is, Jesus Christ, the Head, and we, the members. We offer the life-giving bread and saving cup to give glory to God and to make us holy (cf. *CSL* 7). "It therefore pertains to the whole Body of the Church, manifests it, and has its effect upon it. Indeed, it also affects the individual members of the Church" (*GIRM* 91).

> In the celebration of Mass the faithful form a holy people, a people of God's own possession and a royal Priesthood, so that they may give thanks to God and offer the unblemished sacrificial Victim not only by means of the hands of the Priest but also

together with him and so that they may
learn to offer their very selves (*GIRM* 95).

The Bible urges all of us: "Be holy yourselves in
every aspect of your conduct, for it is written, 'Be holy
because I am holy'" (1 *Pt* 1:15-16). The best source of
our holiness is the Holy Mass. "From the Eucharist,
as from a font, grace is poured forth upon us; and the
sanctification of men in Christ and the glorification
of God, to which all other activities of the Church
are directed as toward their end, is achieved in the
most efficacious possible way" (*CSL* 10). Thus, Pope
Benedict XVI says that the "Eucharist is the root of
every form of holiness" (*SacCar* 94).

With the Prayer over the Offerings (formerly
Prayer over the Gifts), this part of the celebration is
concluded and prepares us for the Eucharistic Prayer,
"the center and high point of the entire celebration"
(*GIRM* 78).

The Eucharistic Prayer

As Jesus *gave thanks* to the Father at the Last Supper,
the Priest also *gives thanks* to the Father "in the
name of the whole of the holy people" (*GIRM* 79a)
at the Eucharistic Prayer, "the prayer of thanksgiving
and sanctification" (*GIRM* 78). For a long time,
Catholics have mainly focused on the Consecration
and elevation of the Host during this prayer. Today,
we have come to appreciate the full context of the
whole prayer which is thanksgiving. That is why it is
called the *Eucharistic* Prayer. Eucharist comes from

the Greek word *Eucharistia* meaning "thanksgiving". Thanksgiving is the context of the entire Eucharistic Prayer. We offer the prayer of praise and thanksgiving over the bread and the wine which become the Body and Blood of Christ for the saving work of God accomplished in Christ's Passion, Death, and Resurrection.

Significantly, the universal Catechism describes the Eucharistic Prayer as "consecratory thanksgiving" (*CCC* 1346) which means that in the act of saying "thank you" to the Father we are at the same time asking him to make sacred all of his creation, the bread and wine, his whole Church, and all her members both living and dead. Saint Justin (A.D. 100-165) said: "Because this bread and wine have been made Eucharist ('eucharisted,' according to an ancient expression), 'we call this food Eucharist'" (*Apol.* 1, 66, 1-2: *PG* 6, 428. Quoted in *CCC* 1355). Thanksgiving is "expressed especially in the Preface" (*GIRM* 79a), which is the very first part of the Eucharistic Prayer.

> **Significantly, the universal Catechism describes the Eucharistic Prayer as "consecratory thanksgiving"** (*CCC* 1346).

It is important to emphasize that the whole Eucharistic Prayer is directed to *God the Father* because we Catholics have been charged by our separated brethren with praying more to the Virgin Mary and the other saints than to God the Creator.

Being *the Great Prayer* of the Church, the Eucharistic Prayer is the great example we can use in explaining that indeed we Catholics *adore* (*latria*) God the Father through Jesus Christ in the Holy Spirit and we *venerate* especially the Virgin Mary (*hyperdulia*) and the other saints (*dulia*). Thus, in the Eucharistic Prayer, we give thanks and pray:

> To you, therefore, most merciful Father, ...
> through Jesus Christ, your Son, our Lord: . . .
> In communion with those whose memory we venerate,
> especially the glorious ever-Virgin Mary, . . .
> and all your Saints; . . .
> in the unity of the Holy Spirit, . . .
> (*Eucharistic Prayer I*).

The major changes in the parts of the people in the Eucharistic Prayer are in the Preface Dialogue, the *Sanctus*, and Memorial Acclamation.

Preface Dialogue

Being the "holy of holies", the Eucharistic Prayer is introduced by the Preface Dialogue with heightened formality and solemnity. As we approach the most important part of the entire celebration of the Holy Mass, the threefold introductory dialogue focuses our attention to the Lord, exhorts us to lift up our hearts to him, and invites us in the act of giving thanks. By keeping this introductory dialogue and literally translating the Latin text into English, the new Roman

Missal has faithfully kept "a most ancient Christian tradition" (Jungmann, II:110). The Preface Dialogue is already evident in the *Apostolic Tradition* (c. 215 A.D.) which is attributed to Saint Hippolytus.

"And with your spirit."

The central part of the entire celebration begins with the greeting "The Lord be with you" to which we reply "And with your spirit." This is the third time we give this response during the Holy Mass. But this time, it acquires its most profound meaning. By our reply, we are recognizing the Priest as truly acting in the person of Christ the Head (*in persona Christi Capitis*) whose body and blood will be made present and offered to the Father by the power of the Holy Spirit and in the process transforming us into his Body, the Church.

Then the Priest exhorts us to lift up our hearts (*Sursum corda*), a phrase that echoes *Lamentations*: "Let us lift up our hearts as well as our hands toward God in heaven!" (3:41). The lifting up of our hearts reminds us of the catechetical definition of prayer as "the raising of one's mind and heart to God" (*CCC* 2590). Although we have surely lifted up our hearts in the preceding prayers, the lifting up of our hearts is especially expressed in the Preface Dialogue of the Eucharistic Prayer because it is *the Great Prayer* of the Church. And if we have not yet really lifted up our hearts in the preceding part of the Holy Mass because of distractions, the exhortation to lift up our hearts at this highest point of the entire celebration of the Holy Mass is very much in order.

This upward movement of prayer is sustained in our response: "We lift them up to the Lord" (*Habemus ad Dominum*). The verb *habemus* means "we hold", i.e., we "hold up and keep held up while the thanksgiving memorial and praise proceed" (Foley, 2011, 261). Commenting on this dialogue, Saint Cyprian (d. 258 A.D.) says:

> Therefore, the priest also before his prayer prepares the minds of the brethren by first uttering a preface, saying: "Lift up your hearts"; so that when the people respond: "We lift them up to the Lord"; they may be admonished that they should ponder on nothing other than the Lord (Defarrari, 1958, 153-154).

"Those who have their minds, hearts, and bodies raised heavenward are ready to offer the true spiritual worship of memorial thanksgiving and so respond that it is right and just to do so" (Foley, 2011, 261-262).

"It is right and just."

The second change in the part of the people in the Eucharistic Prayer is the reply, "It is right and just." This is a literal rendering of the Latin *Dignum et iustum est*. *Dignum* is translated as "right" meaning "fitting," "appropriate," or "worthy." Giving thanks to God is not only doing the correct thing but it also implies that

God is worthy to be given thanks. *Iustum* is translated as "just" meaning "righteous." Thanking God is a righteous act. "In a word, our act of thanking God in the Eucharist is worthy of him (*dignum*) and has a sanctifying or justifying (*iustum*) effect on us" (Foley, 2011, 476). As clearly expressed by Saint Paul in his Second Letter to the *Thessalonians*: "We ought to thank God always for you, brethren, as is fitting" (2 *Thes* 1:3). "For it is surely just on God's part" (2 *Thes* 1:6).

Our reply is affirmed and expanded in the variable Preface which usually begins with these words:

> It is truly right and just, our duty and our salvation,
> always and everywhere to give you thanks,
> Lord, holy Father, almighty and eternal God.

The Preface is concluded with us joining the Priest in singing or saying aloud: the *Sanctus*.

Sanctus

This concluding part of the Preface is called the *Sanctus* (meaning "Holy") because of the triple "holy" that begins the acclamation in which our earthly liturgy is joined with the heavenly liturgy. Joseph Jungmann says that the *Sanctus* "fits best of all in the structure of the eucharistic prayer" (Jungmann, II:133). He explains:

> All of God's benefits and the manifestations of His favor, for which

we must give thanks, are after all only revelations of His inmost being, which is all light and brilliance, inviolable and without stain, before which creation can only bow in deepest reverence—his holiness (Jungmann II:133).

Medieval commentators of the *Sanctus* gave a Trinitarian meaning to the triple "holy" adding that the unity of the Holy Father, the Holy Son, and the Holy Spirit is indicated in the *Dominus Deus* (Lord God).

The new translation has replaced "God of power and might" with "God of hosts."

"God of hosts."

Deus Sabaoth is now literally translated as "God of hosts." *Deus* is a Latin noun which means "God." *Sabaoth* is a Hebrew word which means "hosts." It must first be made clear that the word "hosts" here does not have any connection with the consecrated bread or the Host given at Communion. It is not the Latin *Hostia* but the Hebrew *Sabaoth* which means "hosts" or "armies of angels" understood "in the most ancient tradition a *militia*, which means armies, not choirs, evoking God's power over the universe and against evil" (Foley, 2011, 265). The biblical reference is from *Isaiah* 6:3 ("Holy, holy, holy is the LORD of hosts!" they cried one to the other. "All the earth is filled with his glory!").

Beginning in the mid-sixth century, the *Sanctus* has been joined with the acclamation used by the people to greet Jesus at his entry into Jerusalem. "Hosanna to the Son of David; blessed is he who comes in the name of the Lord; hosanna in the highest" (*Mt* 21:9-10). This second segment of the *Sanctus* is called *Benedictus* (meaning "Blessed"). It expresses the Jewish pilgrim greeting and the messianic expectation: "Blessed is he who comes in the name of the Lord" (*Ps* 118:26). Pope Benedict XVI explains:

> The *Benedictus* also entered the liturgy at a very early stage. For the infant Church, "Palm Sunday" was not a thing of the past. Just as the Lord entered the Holy City that day on a donkey, so too the Church saw him coming again and again in the humble form of bread and wine.
>
> The Church greets the Lord in the Holy Eucharist as the one who is coming now, the one who has entered into her midst. At the same time, she greets him as the one who continues to come, the one who leads us toward his coming. As pilgrims, we go up to him; as a pilgrim, he comes to us and takes us up with him in his "ascent" to the Cross and Resurrection, to the definitive Jerusalem that is already growing in the midst of this world in the communion that unites us with his body (Ratzinger/Benedict XVI, 2011, 10-11).

After joining the angels in heaven worshipping God in eternity and the crowds acclaiming as Jesus entered Jerusalem and now coming to us in the form of bread and wine, we all kneel in humility and adoration. The Priest calls down the Holy Spirit so that the bread and wine may become the Body and Blood of our Lord Jesus Christ and he narrates what happened at the Last Supper.

The *Institution narrative and Consecration* is the "center of the center", the summit and heart of the entire Eucharistic Prayer, because

> by means of the words and actions of Christ, that Sacrifice is effected which Christ himself instituted during the Last Supper, when he offered his Body and Blood under the species of bread and wine, gave them to the Apostles to eat and drink, and leaving with the latter the command to perpetuate this same mystery (*GIRM* 79d).

Immediately after showing us the chalice and genuflecting in adoration, the Priest invites us to respond to the acclamation: "The mystery of faith."

"The mystery of faith."

Consistent with the literal translation of the Latin *Mysterium fidei*, the new Roman Missal simply renders it as "**the mystery of faith**" omitting "Let us proclaim" which was added by the 1973 translation. By doing this, the new Roman Missal has paralleled this announcement with the acclamations at the end of the readings in the Liturgy of the Word ("The Word of the Lord" and "The Gospel of the Lord") and the direct statements in giving Communion ("The Body of Christ" and "The Blood of Christ").

What is "the mystery of faith"? The phrase is found in the Bible, specifically in the First Letter to *Timothy*. Saint Paul says that deacons are to be "holding fast to the mystery of the faith with a clear conscience" (1 *Tim* 3:9). He identifies "the mystery of the faith" in verse 16 of the same Letter:

> Undeniably great is the mystery of devotion,
> Who was manifested in the flesh,
> vindicated in the spirit,
> seen by angels,
> proclaimed to the Gentiles,
> believed in throughout the world,
> taken up in glory.

In the footnote of this verse 16 in the *New American Bible*, it says of the relative pronoun "**Who**: the reference is to Christ, who is himself 'the mystery of our devotion.'" Hence, the content of our belief, "the mystery" of our religion, is Jesus Christ himself.

Why is Jesus Christ called "the mystery"? What is "mystery" in the first place? "Mystery" comes from the Greek *mustērion* meaning "a secret" or "something hidden". Hence, in modern colloquial English, "mystery" refers to something unknown or inexplicable. A mystery story or film arouses our curiosity with heightened suspense because of unknown or hidden facts. In the Bible, "mystery" refers to a truth unknown or hidden to humans but made known to God's holy ones by divine revelation. Saint Paul speaks of "the mystery hidden from ages and from generations past. But now it has been manifested to his holy ones, to whom God chose to make known the riches of the glory of this mystery among the Gentiles; it is Christ in you, the hope for glory" (*Col* 1:26-27).

Jesus Christ is "the mystery" because he reveals what is hidden and incomprehensible to the human mind. He is "the mystery" in whom "there is always more to understand" (cf. *Vatican I, ND* 132). By his words and deeds, he makes known to us God's loving plan of saving us from sin by dying on the cross. "For our paschal lamb, Christ, has been sacrificed" (1 *Cor* 5:7). From the biblical expressions referring to Jesus Christ as "the mystery of the faith" and "Paschal lamb" the rich liturgical and theological term *Paschal Mystery* has eventually evolved as the most significant concept of the Christian faith.

> **Jesus Christ is "the mystery" in whom "there is always more to understand"** (*Vatican I, ND* 132).

The term "Paschal" derives from the Hebrew *Pesach* which means "the passing over." It is applied to the three essentially related events: the Passover meal, the annual feast of the Passover, and the historical Passover of deliverance of the Israelites from death. Before the Israelites left Egypt, the Lord had prescribed the Passover meal (*Ex* 12:1-20), establishing it as an annual "memorial feast" (cf. *Ex* 12:14) to commemorate God's "passing over" the houses of the Israelites whose doorposts and lintel were smeared with the blood of the sacrificed lamb which saved them from death.

In the New Testament, Jesus fulfilled the Jewish "memorial feast" (cf. *Ex* 12:14) at the Last Supper in which he commanded his disciples to "do this in memory of me" (*Lk* 22:19). Christ himself is the Paschal Lamb, "the Lamb of God, who takes away the sin of the world" (*Jn* 1:29). "For our paschal lamb, Christ, has been sacrificed. Therefore let us celebrate the feast" (*1 Cor* 5:7-8). For us Christians, the Jewish celebration of "the LORD's Passover" (*Ex* 12:11) prefigures our celebration of "the Lord's Supper" (1 *Cor* 11:20), the oldest name for the Holy Mass.

Christ's Paschal Mystery, his dying and rising, is the culmination of the "dyings" and "risings" we find in nature, in our secular life, and sacramental life. We see dying when the sun sets in the evening and rising when it shines in the morning. We see dying when oil spills pollute our rivers and rising when environmentalists clean them up. We see dying when our homes are foreclosed and rising when generous people help rebuild our life. We see dying when a soldier leaves his family to defend our freedom and rising when he returns home alive and kicking. We see dying when a young teenager gets hooked in drugs and rising when he is rehabilitated to a new life. We see dying when a doctor tells his patient that he has cancer and rising when his loved ones pitch in for the expenses of the treatment. We see dying when a believer immerses his filthy sins and rising when he is washed clean by the water of Baptism. We see dying when the spouses say the words in Marriage "for worse, for poorer, in sickness" and rising in the words "for better, for richer, and in health". And when we are faced with real, physical death, we get a glimpse of the resurrection when the Priest anoints us with oil and gives us the *Viaticum* (meaning Jesus Christ is "with you on the way" to our heavenly home).

All of these dyings and risings are embraced by the Death and Resurrection of Christ, who is now present in the consecrated bread and wine, the mystery of our faith that we proclaim to the world.

The Three Alternative Acclamations

Before the liturgical reform of Vatican II (1962-1965), the only vocal participation of the people at the Eucharistic Prayer was at the beginning (the Preface Dialogue and the *Sanctus*) and at the end (Amen). The insertion of an acclamation by the people at the high point of the Eucharistic Prayer is one of the greatest achievements of the liturgical reform of Vatican II, which has emphasized active participation of the people.

Happily, the second wave of reform introduced by the third typical edition of *The Roman Missal* did not take away this very significant part of the people in the celebration of the Holy Mass. What was conspicuously deleted was the popular acclamation: "Christ has died, Christ is risen, Christ will come again." Reason: It is not in the original Latin text, although it expresses the same mystery of faith.

The insertion of our acclamation immediately after the Consecration of the bread and wine is not only to increase our participation in the celebration, but also to show the transforming effect Christ's Paschal Mystery in our life and in the entire creation. Pope Benedict XVI says:

> The substantial conversion of bread and wine into his body and blood introduces within creation the principle of a radical change, a sort of "nuclear fission," to use an image familiar to us today, which penetrates to the heart of all being, a change meant to set off a process which transforms reality, a process leading ultimately to the transfiguration of the entire world, to the point where God will be all in all (cf. *1 Cor* 15:28) (*SacCar* 11).

Noticeably, the three choices of acclamations are addressed to Christ although the entire Eucharistic Prayer is directed to the Father. This is not an interruption of the Great Prayer. As we have seen in the *Gloria*, to glorify the Father is to glorify the Son. In the Eucharistic Prayer, to thank the Father is also to thank the Son. Moreover, in the history of the Eucharistic Prayer, "acclamations by the assembly within it are traditionally addressed to Christ" (Hudock, 2010, 77).

All three acclamations express the meaning of "the mystery of faith" which is the Paschal Mystery: Christ's Death and Resurrection. The first two acclamations make reference to the end time (the term employed in theology is "eschatological") as expressed by the words "until you come again." Although our redemption as well as that of the whole world has already been realized in the Death and Resurrection of Christ, we still look forward to its final fulfillment when he comes again. "We know that all creation is groaning in labor pains even until now;

and not only that, but we ourselves, who have the firstfruits of the Spirit, we also groan within ourselves as we wait for adoption, the redemption of our bodies" (*Rom* 8:22-23). That is why we continue to make the petition as expressed in the third acclamation: "Save us, Savior of the world."

"We proclaim your Death, O Lord, and profess your Resurrection until you come again."

This first acclamation as well as the second is inspired by the First Letter to the *Corinthians*: "For as often as you eat this bread and drink the cup, you proclaim the death of the Lord until he comes" (1 *Cor* 11:26). Although Saint Paul mentions only "death" in this biblical passage, the first acclamation adds "Resurrection" thereby completing the whole picture of "the mystery of faith."

Saint Paul says, "If you confess with your mouth that Jesus is Lord and believe in your heart that God raised him from the dead, you will be saved" (*Rom* 10:9). To "confess with your mouth" means to speak, to acknowledge, or to profess openly and publicly. The title "Lord" is used in the New Testament to refer to the risen Christ. "Jesus is Lord" is the oldest and shortest statement of faith of the early Church, the Christian *kerygma* in the New Testament (cf. *CCC* 638). "Therefore let the whole house of Israel know for certain that God has made him both Lord and Messiah, this Jesus whom you crucified" (*Acts* 2:36). "And no one can say, 'Jesus is Lord,' except by the holy Spirit" (1 *Cor* 12:3). "For we do not preach ourselves but Jesus Christ as Lord" (2 *Cor* 4:5). In professing that "Christ is Lord", the early Christians suffered for their belief but at the same time experienced deep joy in their liturgy singing and proclaiming Jesus Christ

> Who, though he was in the form of God,
> did not regard equality with God
> something to be grasped.
> Rather, he emptied himself,
> taking the form of a slave,
> coming in human likeness;
> and found human in appearance,
> he humbled himself,
> becoming obedient to death, even death on
> a cross.
> Because of this, God greatly exalted him
> and bestowed on him the name
> that is above every name,
> that at the name of Jesus
> every knee should bend,
> of those in heaven and on earth and under
> the earth,
> and every tongue confess that
> Jesus Christ is Lord (*Phil* 2:6-11).

Therefore, the proclamation of Christ's Death and Resurrection is a "profession of faith." In fact, it is not only the Memorial Acclamation that is considered as "profession of faith" but also the entire Eucharistic Prayer. Jungmann says that "in the most ancient tradition the *eucharistia* appears at the same time as another more exalted form of the profession of faith" (Jungmann, II:117).

> **"In the most ancient tradition the *eucharistia* appears at the same time as another more exalted form of the profession of faith"** (Jungmann, II:117).

It is beyond the scope of this book to discuss the studies made by experts showing the parallelism between the Creed and the Eucharistic Prayer (cf. Mazza, 1986, 159-160). It is sufficient to point out that the Eucharistic Prayer is a profession of faith not only in words but also in action. What is being professed in words is also being performed in action. In fact, the ancient sacramentaries of the sixth century and the *Ordines Romani* that describe the celebration of the Holy Mass between the seventh and fourteenth centuries use the word "Action" to refer to the Eucharistic Prayer. The heading of the Preface Dialogue indicates: *Incipit canon actionis* (The canon of the action begins). This is similar to what the director tells the whole crew and the actors in video or film production. Once everyone is ready to shoot, the director shouts: "Action!"

Significantly, it is worth mentioning that today the Order of Mass of the third typical edition of *The Roman Missal* mentions "Action" in Eucharistic Prayer I (The Roman Canon). In paragraph no. 86, it inserts the rubric between the Commemoration of the Living and the *Communicantes* (Communion with the

Saints): "Within the Action." The Eucharistic Prayer is *the* Action of the Church. Our social actions, our apostolic works for the poor, for human rights, for the environment, and our Bible apostolate and religious practices and devotions culminate and draw their source from the Holy Mass particularly from its Great Prayer, from its Great Action, the Eucharistic Prayer.

"When we eat this Bread and drink this Cup, we proclaim your Death, O Lord, until you come again."

The English saying "Action speaks louder than words" has been most eloquently proven true by Christ in his sacrificial Action of dying on the cross. Indeed, "Action is eloquence", says William Shakespeare. "No one has greater love than this, to lay down one's life for one's friends" (*Jn* 15:13). Jesus said this at the Last Supper in which he has given us his body and blood: "This is my body, which will be given for you" and "This cup is the new covenant in my blood, which will be shed for you" (*Lk* 22:19-20). The next day, true to his words, Jesus gave up his body and blood for us on the cross.

Today, Christ continues to give his body and blood for us at the Holy Mass. "For as often as you eat this bread and drink the cup, you proclaim the death of the Lord until he comes" (1 *Cor* 11:26). The Action of Christ, his sacrificial Death on the cross, is made present in our Action of eating the consecrated Bread and drinking the consecrated Wine until he comes again. The proclamation of the Death of Christ is "to be understood as a profession of faith in which we confess the death of Christ as a mystery of salvation" (Mazza, 1986, 160).

The separation of the Bread from the Wine has been interpreted as a portrayal of the sacrificial aspect of the Holy Mass. It has been explained that since the Bread is the Body of Christ and the Wine is the Blood of Christ, their separation in the Eucharistic celebration points to Christ's Death on the cross where he shed his blood.

While this is a pious explanation that may deepen our spiritual reflection on the Holy Mass as Sacrifice, it must be emphasized that this is an allegorical interpretation. It has no basis on history and liturgy. A more accurate explanation that is not only historical but also theological and liturgical is that the Holy Mass is a *sacrificial meal*. The Last Supper was celebrated by Christ in anticipation of his impending Death. Our Eucharist is a commemoration of Christ's Death on the cross and the victory of his Resurrection in the context of a meal. As Father Chupungco has clearly distinguished, what we must separate is the theological content from the liturgical shape of the Eucharist. The liturgical shape is the ritual meal; its theological content, Christ's sacrificial death on the cross (cf. Chupungco, 1989, 71-77).

According to then Cardinal Ratzinger, the meaning of the Death of Jesus on the cross is expressed by Saint John in his gospel: "And when I am lifted up from the earth, I will draw everyone to myself" (*Jn* 12:32). He explains that the crucifixion is "a process of opening" in which the scattered humans "are drawn into the embrace of Jesus Christ, into the wide span of his outstretched arms . . . Christ is the completely open man, in whom the dividing walls of existence are torn down, who is entirely 'transition' (Passover, 'Pasch')" (Ratzinger, 2004, 240).

The complete openness of Jesus on the cross is most vividly portrayed in the picture of his pierced side. "One soldier thrust his lance into his side, and immediately blood and water flowed out" (*Jn* 19:34). The piercing of his side is the last blow that puts a period on Jesus' life on earth. Hanging on the tree of the cross with outstretched arms, Jesus Christ is now the new Adam from whose side Eve, a new humankind, is formed. The pierced side of the new Adam recalls the "open side" of man at creation: it is the beginning of a new community, "a community symbolized here by blood and water, in which John points to the basic Christian sacraments of baptism and Eucharist and, through them, to the Church" (Ratzinger, 2004, 241).

> **"One soldier thrust his lance into his side, and immediately blood and water flowed out"** (*Jn* 19:34).

"Save us, Savior of the world, for by your Cross and Resurrection you have set us free."

In this third choice for the acclamation, we express the petition: "Save us, Savior of the world". The name Jesus means "God is salvation". His title as "Savior of the world" is taken from *John* 4:42 in which the Samaritans say to the woman whom Jesus meets at the well, "We no longer believe because of your word; for we have heard for ourselves, and we know that this is truly the savior of the world" (*Jn* 4:42). This statement of belief of the Samaritans is the climax of the story of the faith journey of the Samaritan woman.

The story begins with Jesus, a Jew, asking for water from a woman, a Samaritan. At that time, Jews and Samaritans were racial enemies. This is the background why the Samaritan woman said to Jesus, "How can you, a Jew, ask me, a Samaritan woman, for a drink?" (*Jn* 4:9). Also, women then were considered second class citizens. This is the reason why the disciples "were amazed that he was talking with a woman" (*Jn* 4:27). Breaking down racial and gender prejudice, Jesus initiates a dialogue with the Samaritan woman and gradually reveals himself to her.

After Jesus promises to give her "the living water" (*Jn* 4:10), the woman addresses him as "Sir" (*Jn* 4:15). After Jesus reveals his knowledge of her having several men in her life, the woman calls Jesus a "prophet" (*Jn* 4:19). After Jesus says to her that "salvation is from the Jews" (*Jn* 4:22) and that "God is Spirit, and those who worship him must worship in Spirit and truth" (*Jn* 4:24), the woman calls him the "Messiah" (*Jn* 4:29) and started testifying, "He told me everything I have done" (*Jn* 4:39). Finally, after the Samaritans have heard Jesus himself (Cf. *Jn* 4:41), they profess the faith that he is "the Savior of the world" (*Jn* 4:42).

Step by step Jesus Christ has revealed himself to the Samaritan woman who gives her corresponding assent of faith in Jesus. Thus, the woman comes to know him first as a "Jew", then she calls him "sir", "prophet", "Messiah", and finally "Savior of the world". Also, the faith of the Samaritans has moved from the word of the woman to the word of Jesus himself whom they, like the Samaritan woman, have encountered personally.

Step by step Jesus Christ is also guiding us like the Samaritan woman in our faith journey. Today many of us confess that Jesus is their personal Savior. They make their own the personal experience of Saint Paul, "I live, no longer I, but Christ lives in me; insofar as I now live in the flesh, I live by faith in the Son of God who has loved me and given himself up for me" (*Gal* 2:20).

Acclaiming Jesus as "Savior of the world", we proclaim that he will save this earth from environmental crisis by giving us "a spring of water welling up to eternal life" (*Jn* 4:14). We proclaim that through dialogue Jesus Christ will break down the walls of division, discrimination, and intolerance. We proclaim that if you will "worship in Spirit and truth" (*Jn* 4:24), you will "live by the Spirit and you will certainly not gratify the desire of the flesh" (*Gal* 5:16). We proclaim that Jesus Christ is not only the Savior of the Jews (Messiah) but the Savior of all people: Jews and Samaritans, Christians and Gentiles, Greeks and Romans, Americans and Chinese, men and women, sinners and saints, gays and lesbians. "For freedom Christ set us free; so stand firm and do not submit again to the yoke of slavery" (*Gal* 5:1).

Thus, the Memorial Acclamation is the proclamation of our faith in the Paschal Mystery of

Christ in which we and the whole creation participate. In the words of Blessed John Paul II:

> The Paschal Mystery of Christ is the full revelation of the mystery of the world's origin, the climax of the history of salvation and the anticipation of the eschatological fulfilment of the world. What God accomplished in Creation and wrought for his People in the Exodus has found its fullest expression in Christ's Death and Resurrection, though its definitive fulfilment will not come until the Parousia, when Christ returns in glory (*Dies Domini* 18).

After the Memorial Acclamation, the Priest continues the Eucharistic Prayer and we listen "to it with reverence and in silence" (*GIRM* 78) . . . remembering, offering, asking for intercessions, and glorifying the Father, the Son, and the Holy Spirit. We respond to the Great Prayer with the Great Amen.

"Amen."

Amen is a Hebrew word which means "so be it, truly, verily." It has remained untranslated in the Greek Bible (*Septuagint*) and in the Liturgy of the Church. In the Old Testament, *Amen* was the congregational response of the people to express their agreement and affirmation to the proclamation of the word. "Ezra opened the scroll so that all the people might see it (for he was standing higher up than any of the people); and, as he opened it, all the people rose. Ezra blessed the LORD, the great God, and all the people, their hands raised high, answered, 'Amen, amen!' Then they bowed down and prostrated themselves before the LORD, their faces to the ground" (*Neh* 8:5-6).

In the New Testament, our Lord Jesus Christ himself frequently said *Amen*: twenty-eight times in Saint Matthew's gospel and twenty-six times in its doubled form in Saint John's. Jesus affirms the truthfulness of his words by beginning his statements with *Amen*. "Jesus said to them, 'Amen, amen, I say to you, before Abraham came to be, I AM'" (*Jn* 8:58).

Like Jesus, Saint Paul frequently used *Amen* in his letters (cf. *Rom* 1:25; 9:5; 11:36; 16:27; 2 *Cor* 1:20; *Gal* 1:5; *Eph* 3:21; *Phil* 4:20; 1 *Tim* 1:17; 6:16; 2 *Tim* 4:18). He urged the use of the Hebrew *Amen* in the liturgical services of the churches he founded even though those churches did not know Hebrew. For example, in answering the problem of praying in a foreign tongue put forward to him by the Greek-speaking church in Corinth, he asked, "How shall one who holds the place of the uninstructed say the 'Amen' to your thanksgiving, since he does not know what you are saying?" (1 *Cor* 14:16). Saint Paul usually ended his praise and glory to God with *Amen*. "For from him and through him and for him are all things. To him be glory forever. Amen" (*Rom* 11:36).

Because of the frequent use of *Amen* by Jesus and Saint Paul, the Church has perpetuated it in our liturgical celebrations. Today, we say *Amen* at least nine times in the course of the celebration of the Holy

Mass. Our *Amen* at the end of the Eucharistic Prayer is the most significant. It is our great affirmation to the Great Prayer.

Father Paul Turner shares a contemporary explanation of our Great Amen. He says that a child compares the Great Amen to e-mail, "It's like hitting 'Send'." Father Turner agrees, "Indeed. We send our entire message all at once through the angelic Web server to the in-box of the one who rules over all" (Turner, 2010, 35).

The Communion Rite

The Eucharistic Prayer, which consists of several prayers, is treated as one unit because all its subunits are performed in the context of the one thanksgiving. Similarly, the Communion Rite is also considered as one unit, being in the singular form (not Communion Rites), because its subunits are "preparatory rites by which the faithful are led more immediately to Communion" (*GIRM* 81).

The Lord's Prayer, the Rite of Peace, and the Fraction (Breaking) of the Bread are like steps of a ladder that lead us to the highest rung of our participation in the celebration of the Holy Mass: receiving the Eucharistic Bread and Wine in Holy Communion.

The Lord's Prayer

Being the prayer given to us by Jesus, the Lord's Prayer is the best link between the Eucharistic Prayer and the Communion Rite. Its first part serves as a "sort of summary and recapitulation of the preceding eucharistic prayer" (Jungmannn, II:279) and its second part prepares us for Communion.

The first petition "hallowed be thy name" recalls the triple "holy" of the *Sanctus*; "thy kingdom come", the calling down of the Holy Spirit (*epiclesis*); and "thy will be done" "sets forth the basic idea regarding obedience from which all sacrifice must proceed" (Jungmann, II:279).

The second part of the Our Father expresses a petition "for daily food, which for Christians means principally the Eucharistic Bread, and entreating also purification from sin, so that what is holy may in truth be given to the holy" (*GIRM* 81). The Eucharist has been our "daily bread" which we can only receive worthily if we feel that we are forgiven our sins, free from all evil, and at peace with God, with ourselves, and with our brothers and sisters.

At this point, the changes in the part of the people are in the responses to the greeting of peace and the prayer before Communion.

The Rite of Peace

"And with your spirit."

For the fourth time, we say the response "And with your spirit." But at this particular part of the celebration, it is a reply to the Priest's greeting of peace. The reciprocal greeting signals the announcement and the act of exchanging the sign of peace.

The peace that we wish for each other is the peace that comes from the risen Christ. This is the reason for the present position of the rite. "The peace offered to the apostles after the resurrection in John's Gospel derives from the sacrificial death and resurrection of the Lord" (Francis and Pecklers, 2000, 105). Thus, after recognizing the Lord in the Eucharistic Sacrifice, "the Church entreats peace and unity for herself and for the whole human family, and the faithful express to each other their ecclesial communion and mutual charity before communicating in the Sacrament" (*GIRM* 82).

"Ecclesial communion and mutual charity" are what Saint Paul requires in the celebration of "the Lord's Supper". For lack of peace in the Corinthian community, Saint Paul chides them, "I hear that when you meet as a church there are divisions among you . . . When you meet in one place, then, it is not to eat the Lord's supper, for in eating, each one goes ahead with his own supper, and one goes hungry while another gets drunk" (*1 Cor* 11:18, 20-21).

Clearly, then, our exchange of peace before Holy Communion has ethical demands. Our union with Jesus Christ implies that we are at peace with our brothers and sisters. It is hypocrisy if we exchange peace with one another, but we have not forgiven our disobedient children. It is hypocrisy if we exchange peace with one another, but we have not reconciled with our mother-in-law. It is hypocrisy if we exchange peace with one another, but we have not given just wages to our employees. "Giving each other a sign of peace, then, is a pledge to do all we can to bring forgiveness and reconciliation wherever it is needed: within families, cities, nations, our whole world" (Foley, 2011, 617).

The Fraction of the Bread

As Christ *broke* the bread at the Last Supper, the Priest also *breaks* the Eucharistic Bread at the Holy Mass. The act of breaking is accompanied by the invocation *Agnus Dei* (Lamb of God). The wordings of the *Agnus Dei* remain the same. We recall the announcement of Saint John the Baptist at the Jordan River: "Behold, the Lamb of God, who takes away the sin of the world" (*Jn* 1:29). These words are echoed by the Priest as he shows us the Host "holding it slightly raised above the paten or above the chalice" (*Order of Mass* 132): "Behold the Lamb of God, behold him who takes away the sins of the world." The word "behold" also reminds us of the words of Pilate to the crowd presenting the tortured body of Jesus: "Behold, the man!" ("*Ecce homo*") (*Jn* 19:5).

As we "behold" the Host, we see the Sacrificial Victim, the scourged body of Jesus Christ, the broken bread. We also see the broken world, the broken ground, the broken industry, the broken hearts, and the broken homes. That is why we plead, "Have mercy on us." At this periods of distress, we ask, "Grant us peace."

If this is the picture that we see at this part of the Holy Mass, is it still appropriate to sing a joyful melody of the *Agnus Dei* with the clapping of hands and the swaying of bodies? "In the East it had become the practice since the sixth century to regard the breaking of the species of bread as a reference to our Lord's Passion and death" (Jungmann, II:334). This theology of the fraction has not changed. As Father Paul Turner says, "The breaking of bread reminds the community of the Passover lamb, slaughtered for the salvation of God's chosen people" (Turner, 2012, 129).

The Lamb of God who will be our food in Holy Communion is also the triumphant Lamb in the book of Revelation. We look forward to participate in the heavenly banquet of the Lamb. "Blessed are those who have been called to the wedding feast of the Lamb" (*Rev* 19:9). In the earthly liturgy, the Priest invites us to "the supper of the Lamb." He says, "Blessed are those called to the supper of the Lamb." Our Holy Communion is a foretaste of the "wedding feast of the Lamb", the marriage of Christ, the Lamb, and his bride, the Church (cf. 2 *Cor* 11:2; *Eph* 5:22-27). This will take place at the end of the world. Then we will "rejoice and be glad and give him glory. For the wedding day of the Lamb has come, his bride has made herself ready" (*Rev* 19:7). But while we are still here wandering in the valley of tears, in this broken world with its broken promises, we humbly pray, "Lord, I am not worthy".

"That you should enter under my roof, but only say the word and my soul shall be healed."

Domine, non sum dignus, ut intres sub tectum meum is now literally translated as "Lord, I am not worthy **that you should enter under my roof**" replacing "Lord, I am not worthy to receive you". The reason for the change is of course faithfulness to the Latin text and its biblical reference. This is another instance where a literal translation requires explanation.

After the Priest invites us to "the supper of the Lamb", together with us "he makes an act of humility, using the prescribed words from the Gospels" (*GIRM* 84). The new "prescribed words" in the liturgy are:

> Lord, I am not worthy
> that you should enter under my roof,
> but only say the word
> and my soul shall be healed.

This prayer before Communion is an adaptation of the words of the Roman centurion or general from the Gospels of Matthew and Luke. "Lord, I am not worthy to have you enter under my roof; only say the word and my servant will be healed" (*Mt* 8:8; cf. *Lk* 7:6-7).

The most significant point in the prayer is not the "roof" but the attitude of humility and faith of the Roman centurion. He asks Jesus to heal his servant. But because of his feeling of unworthiness to receive Jesus in his house, he expresses his strong faith. He firmly believes that by the great power of Christ's word his servant will be healed instantly and distantly. Like the Roman centurion, we do not deserve Jesus because of our sins. We need the centurion's sincere humility and strong faith before receiving Jesus Christ in Holy Communion.

However, since the concrete and vivid image of "roof" strikes us in our prayer, it may be helpful to recall the poetic words of Christ who himself uses the image of entering a house to express his wish of seeking fellowship with us: "Behold, I stand at the door and knock. If anyone hears my voice and opens the door, [then] I will enter his house and dine with him, and he with me" (*Rev* 3:20).

The change from "**I** shall be healed" to "**my soul** shall be healed" *(sanabitur anima mea)* is not to be interpreted to mean that only the spiritual dimension of our being receives the healing effect of Communion. Christ heals the whole human person by directly dealing with the root cause of all sickness: the brokenness within each of us. "The roots of sickness go much deeper than the physical" (15), says Father Teo S. Rustia, spiritual director of the Spirit of Love Covenanted Community, in his book on healing, *Rx Prayer: How Prayer Always Heals*.

> The brokenness of the human person lies as a substratum of the life of mankind, wars, pestilence, global warming, ecological destruction. The ill effects of modern civilization are precisely effects. Their common denominator is the brokenness within the human person (3).

The new translation indicates the radical and complete effect of the healing process brought about by receiving the Body and Blood of our Lord Jesus Christ. If Communion is truly "the medicine of immortality," it heals our soul, which is the "seed of eternity we bear in ourselves, irreducible to the merely material" (*CCC* 33; cf. *GS* 18 § 1).

Communion

As Jesus *gave* his Body and Blood to his disciples at the Last Supper, the Priest *gives* us the consecrated bread and wine in Holy Communion. We are now most intimately united with Jesus Christ, who heals and saves us from stress, sickness, and death. By our singing together, processing together, and individually receiving Jesus Christ we are transformed into his Body, the Church.

Prayer after Communion

The Prayer after Communion has a twofold function: "To bring to completion the prayer of the People of God, and also to conclude the whole Communion Rite" (*GIRM* 89). Our individual prayers remain incomplete in the Holy Mass if they are "not publicly united with the prayers and needs" of the other members of our community "in communion with a universal Church" (Foley, 2011, 192).

Similar to the Collect of the Introductory Rites, the Prayer after Communion gathers our individual needs and prayers which we say in silence after the Priest invites us to pray. If silence has just been observed before the Priest says "Let us pray", the Priest starts praying "for the fruits of the mystery just celebrated" (*GIRM* 89). Thus, the Prayer after Communion is not a prayer of thanksgiving which has already been prayed at the Eucharistic Prayer. It is a prayer of petition for the fruits of Holy Communion.

Fruits of Holy Communion

The Prayer after Communion expresses the fruits that we are to bring to our homes, schools, offices, department stores, and the world. The fruits of receiving Holy Communion are also identified by the universal catechism:

(1) "Communion . . . preserves, increases, and renews the life of grace received at Baptism" (*CCC* 1392);

(2) "Holy Communion separates us from sin" (*CCC* 1393);

(3) "The Eucharist strengthens our charity, which tends to be weakened in daily life; and this living charity wipes away venial sins" (*CCC* 1394);

(4) "The Eucharist preserves us from future mortal sins" (*CCC* 1395);

(5) "The Eucharist makes the Church" (*CCC* 1396);

(6) "The Eucharist commits us to the poor" (*CCC* 1397).

All these fruits of Holy Communion flow from the principal fruit which "is an intimate union with Christ Jesus" (*CCC* 1391). "Whoever eats my flesh and drinks my blood remains in me and I in him" (*Jn* 6:56).

When each of us receives Christ in Communion, our union with him is not an exclusive union as in the union of husband and wife. The marital love of the spouses excludes other men and women. Our union with Jesus is an inclusive union of the branches with the Vine. "I am the vine, you are the branches. Whoever remains in me and I in him will bear much fruit, because without me you can do nothing" (*Jn* 15:5). We are the individual branches that are united with the Vine who is Jesus Christ. We all remain in the one Vine in Holy Communion.

We have long thought of Communion as assimilating Jesus inside us just as we digest food in our internal organs. On the contrary, it is our individual selves that are assimilated and transformed by Communion. This is the constant teaching of Pope Benedict XVI that can be traced back when he was Cardinal Ratzinger.

In his 1991 book *Zur Gemeinschaft gerufen: Kirche heute verstehen* which was translated into English in 1996 (*Called to Communion: Understanding the Church Today*), then Joseph Cardinal Ratzinger said:

> Communion means the fusion of existences; just as in the taking of nourishment the body assimilates foreign matter to itself, and is thereby enabled to live, in the same way my "I" is "assimilated" to that of Jesus, it is made similar to him in an exchange that increasingly breaks through the lines of division. This same event takes place in the case of all who communicate; they are all assimilated to this "bread" and thus are made one among themselves—*one* body (1996, 36-37).

In his first encyclical letter in 2005, *Deus est Caritas* (God is Love), Pope Benedict XVI says:

> In sacramental communion I become one with the Lord, like all the other communicants. As Saint Paul says, "Because there is one bread, we who are many are one body, for we all partake of the one bread" (*1 Cor* 10:17). Union with Christ is also union with all those to whom he gives himself. I cannot possess Christ just for myself; I can belong to him only in union with all those who have become, or who will become, his own. Communion draws me out of myself towards him, and thus also towards unity with all Christians. We become "one body", completely joined in a single existence. Love of God and love of neighbour are now truly united: God incarnate draws us all to himself (14).

And in 2007, Pope Benedict XVI writes in his first post-synodal apostolic exhortation *Sacramentum Caritatis* (The Sacrament of Charity):

> It is not the eucharistic food that is changed into us, but rather we who are mysteriously transformed by it. Christ nourishes us by uniting us to himself; "he draws us into himself" (70).

This truth is echoed by Pope Francis who says:

The Eucharist is the sacrament of communion, which brings us out from individualism to live together our journey in His footsteps, our faith in Him. We ought, therefore, to ask ourselves before the Lord: How do I live the Eucharist? Do I live it anonymously or as a moment of true communion with the Lord, [and] also with many brothers and sisters who share this same table? (Homily for Corpus Christi, May 30, 2013: http://www.news.va/en/news/pope-homily-for-corpus-christi-full-text).

For this reason, one of the names for the Eucharist is "*Holy Communion*, because by this sacrament we unite ourselves to Christ who makes us sharers in his Body and Blood to form a single body" (*CCC* 1331).

D. The Concluding Rites

The Concluding Rites consist of *brief* announcements, the Priest's Greeting and Blessing, the Dismissal, and reverence to the altar. They are clearly brief, but they play a crucial role. They serve as link between our sacramental life and our secular life.

For the last time, the Priest addresses us "The Lord be with you" and we reply "And with your spirit."

"And with your spirit."

It seems strange that we still make an exchange of greeting with the Priest at the end of the Eucharistic celebration. This should not really surprise us because Saint Paul himself uses the greeting to end his letters: "The grace of the Lord Jesus Christ be with your spirit" (*Phil* 4:23; cf. *Gal* 6:18; *Phlm* 25; 2 *Tim* 4:22). What is the purpose of the greeting at this concluding part of the Holy Mass?

We have seen the dialogue, "The Lord be with you" "And with your spirit", at the beginning of the key moments of the celebration. The dialogue does not only call our attention to, and make us aware of, the Lord's presence in the assembly, but it also signals that something new is about to happen to us. At the very beginning of the Holy Mass, the reciprocal greeting signals that we are being formed into a worshipping community as the Body of Christ. At the Gospel, the dialogue signals that Christ will be proclaiming his good news to us, his Church, here and now. At the beginning of the Preface, the exchange of greeting signals the consecratory thanksgiving prayer that will transform the bread and wine into the Body and Blood of Christ and our transformation into Christ's very own Body.

Now at the Concluding Rites, the dialogue "signals that the assembly is about to begin a new phase in its worship—the shift from one context to another, from worship within the church to living out one's Christian commitment in all other aspects of one's life" (Foley, 2011, 636).

Just as Christ has been present throughout the entire celebration of the Holy Mass, we are assured that he is also present with us as we go and "leave" the church building to "live" the Holy Mass. As we prepare to move to this new phase of our worship, the Prayers after Mass on pages 124-128 are provided to help us transition and live our own Pasch. The last exchange of greeting, "The Lord be with you" "And with your spirit", simply means that we are not alone as we are sent. The Lord Jesus is with us.

As soldiers are sent into the battlefield with weapons in their arms, we are sent into the world to be missionaries carrying the blessing of the cross and the words of thanksgiving (Eucharist) in our hearts. In the past, many Catholics thought of "missionaries" as referring only to priests and religious men and women who were sent to "foreign missions". Today, all Catholics are called to be "missionaries". We are all challenged to spread the faith in all circumstances of our life. This is the meaning when the Priest dismisses us with the words, "Go and announce the Gospel of the Lord."

This dismissal formula clearly expresses the essential relationship between Eucharist and mission. The missionary sense is expressed by the Latin *Ite* ("Go") which is the common beginning of the four alternative dismissal formulas of the new English translation of the Order of Mass. "Go" is a strong imperative that reminds us of Christ's missionary mandate, "Go, therefore, and make disciples of all nations, baptizing them in the name of the Father, and of the Son, and of the holy Spirit, teaching them to observe all that I have commanded you. And behold,

I am with you always, until the end of the age" (*Mt* 28:19-20).

The command to "announce the Gospel of the Lord" is the meaning of "evangelization". Pope Benedict XVI has constantly called upon all Catholics to participate in a *New Evangelization* of the world. *New Evangelization* is a favorite theme of his pontificate. He even created the *Pontifical Council for Promoting the New Evangelization* on September 21, 2010. And in his October 7, 2012 homily during the Holy Mass for the opening of the Synod of Bishops on the theme *The New Evangelization for the Transmission of the Christian Faith*, Pope Benedict XVI specified the focus of the *New Evangelization*. It is "directed principally at those who, though baptized, have drifted away from the Church and live without reference to the Christian life" (http://www.vatican.va/holy_father/benedict_xvi/homilies/2012/documents/hf_ben-xvi_hom_20121007_apertura-sinodo_en.html). The *New Evangelization* asks each of us for an authentic renewal of our faith, joy, and love of Christ. As Pope Benedict XVI says, "'*Caritas Christi urget nos'* (*2 Cor* 5:14): it is the love of Christ that fills our hearts and impels us to evangelize. Today as in the past, he sends us through the highways of the world to proclaim his Gospel to all the peoples of the earth (cf. *Mt* 28:19)" (*PF* 7).

To recap, let us borrow the A-L-T-A-R prayer which Father Jerry Orbos, SVD, recommends for our private prayers (cf. Orbos, 2007, January 29) and let us adopt it to our public prayer. The entire Holy Mass is *the* A-L-T-A-R Prayer from which all our prayers and devotions flow and to which they are all directed. At the Holy Mass, the Lord calls us together and assembles us as his one people beginning with the Introductory Rites to:

A—Adore God the Father through his Son Jesus Christ in the Holy Spirit with a sacred language that fosters respect and expresses our Catholic faith; at the Liturgy of the Word, he invites us to

L—Listen to his word as he speaks to us through the proclamation of the Scriptures; at the Liturgy of the Eucharist, he exhorts us to

T—Thank him for his gift of creation and salvation transforming the bread and wine into the Body and Blood of his Son Jesus Christ and transforming us into Christ's Mystical Body; at the Communion Rite, we

A—Ask the Lord that the fruits of receiving him in Communion may bear fruit in our secular life and bring us to eternal life; and at the Concluding Rites, we are sent to live the Mass as we

R—Rejoice in the Lord because he has assured us that he is always with us today, always, and forever.

Chapter III

"THE SAME MASS"

Despite some changes to the Holy Mass, it is **the same Mass** that the Church has been celebrating since Christ commanded his disciples to "do this in memory of me" because it is . . .

The Memorial of Jesus

The Holy Mass has been celebrated by the Church as a Memorial. It is a commemoration of Christ's Passion, Death, and Resurrection.

In the introductory part of the preceding chapter, we have likened the Holy Mass to the Memorial Day celebration in the United States. While we could make this comparison, we must note at this point that the Holy Mass is vastly different from the U.S Memorial Day because Memorial is differently understood in the Liturgy. The Eucharist is not a gathering around the dead or cold monument, but a celebration of the reality of Jesus Christ's dying and rising around the Lord's table.

In the Bible, when the Jews commemorate the saving deeds of God, they do not only recall the past events but the past events become present and real. Their Memorial celebration is like a time-machine that brings the past event to the present moment.

> In the sense of Sacred Scripture the memorial is not merely the recollection of past events but the proclamation of the mighty works wrought by God for men. In the liturgical celebration of these events, they become in a certain way present and real. This is how Israel understands its liberation from Egypt: every time Passover is celebrated, the Exodus events are made present to the memory of believers so that they may conform their lives to them (*CCC* 1363).

When they "re-member" the Passover event, the Jews become participants of the liberation from slavery in Egypt to freedom in the Promised Land. Etymologically, the word "remember" could have come either from the Latin *re-membrum* (*re*—again; *membrum*—limb, part) or "*re-memorārī*" (*re*—again; *memor*—mindful). In "re-membering" the Passover, Israel is not only "mindful again" of the marvelous, saving deeds of God, but Israel becomes "part again" (*re-membrum*) of those past events. Like a "limb" (*membrum*), Israel remains really connected to the main "body" of the celebration, i.e., the actual, present, and real event of the Passover.

As a Jew, Jesus carries on the same Jewish understanding of Memorial when he says, "Do this in memory of me." Being the definitive fulfillment of the Passover, Jesus is telling us that when we celebrate the Eucharist, we become present at the culminating events of his saving work at the Last Supper anticipating his death, at Calvary destroying death, and on his resurrection restoring our life. This is the theological meaning of the word "today" in the Liturgy.

The Real Presence of the Body of Christ

It is the same Mass because it is a celebration of the Real Presence of the Body of Christ. When we "re-member" and celebrate Christ's redemptive act of liberating us from sin, we really join him in passing from death to life because we are His Body and He is the Head of the Body. The physical body of Christ that presided at the Last Supper on Holy Thursday and offered on the Cross on Good Friday and became glorious on Easter Sunday is truly, really, and substantially present "today" in His Mystical Body, that is, the Church. When we pray and sing together, we manifest that we are One Body of Christ. As Saint Paul says, "The cup of blessing that we bless, is it not a participation in the blood of Christ? The bread that we break, is it not a participation in the body of Christ? Because the loaf of bread is one, we, though many, are one body, for we all partake of the one loaf" (1 *Cor* 10:16-17).

> Indeed, Jesus Christ himself is present in our celebration of the Mass. He is present in the sacrifice of the Mass, not only in the person of His minister, "the same now offering, through the ministry of priests, who formerly offered himself on the cross", but especially under the eucharistic species. . . . He is present in His word, since it is He Himself who speaks when the holy scriptures are read in the Church (*CSL* 7).

The Mass that we celebrate today is the same Mass that has been celebrated by Christ two thousand years ago. It is the same Mass because of Christ Himself who promised: "Where two or three are gathered together in my name, there am I in the midst of them" (*Mt* 18:20).

The Sacrament of Christ

It is the same Mass because it is Christ himself who acts in the Sacrament of the Holy Mass that is celebrated "*ex opere operato* (literally: 'by the very fact of the action's being performed'), i.e., by virtue of the saving work of Christ, accomplished once for all" (*CCC* 1128).

In the language of this information age, Christ had already "prepaid" our salvation with his suffering and death and resurrection, offering us unlimited line of communication to eternity. As Saint John says, "In this is love: not that we have loved God, but that he loved us and sent his Son as expiation for our sins. . . . We love because he first loved us" (1 *Jn* 4:10 and19). For this reason, Saint Augustine calls the Eucharist "a sacrament of love, a sign of unity, a bond of charity" (cf. *CSL* 47).

> **"It is the whole community,**
> **the Body of Christ united with**
> **its Head, that celebrates"**
> (*CCC* 1140).

Therefore, despite the changes to the Holy Mass, it is the same Mass because it is Christ himself who celebrates the Mass. It is His whole Body, that is, Christ the Head and we the members, who celebrates the Mass as Memorial and Sacrament of Christ's Sacrifice on the cross. As the *Catechism of the Catholic Church* puts it: "It is the whole community, the Body of Christ united with its Head, that celebrates" (1140).

The Sacrifice of Christ

It is the same Mass because "the sacrifice of Christ and the sacrifice of the Eucharist are ***one single sacrifice*** *(CCC* 1367). "From the first community of Jerusalem until the parousia, it is the same Paschal mystery that the Churches of God, faithful to the apostolic faith, celebrate in every place" (*CCC* 1200).

How can this be? How can the two become "one single sacrifice"? The Sacrifice of Christ and the

Sacrifice of the Eucharist form "one single sacrifice" because it is the same Christ, the one Mediator between God and man, who offers himself in both Sacrifice on the cross and Sacrifice on the table. Echoing the teaching formulated by the Council of Trent, the universal Catechism says:

> "The victim is one and the same: the same now offers through the ministry of priests, who then offered himself on the cross; only the manner of offering is different." "And since in this divine sacrifice which is celebrated in the Mass, the same Christ who offered himself once in a bloody manner on the altar of the cross is contained and is offered in an unbloody manner . . . this sacrifice is truly propitiatory" (*CCC* 1367).

Christ died on the cross once and for all. "He died to sin once and for all" (*Rom* 6:10). "He has no need, as did the high priests, to offer sacrifice day after day, . . . he did that once for all when he offered himself" (*Heb* 7:27). "He entered once for all into the sanctuary, not with the blood of goats and calves but with his own blood, thus obtaining eternal redemption" (*Heb* 9:12). This Sacrifice of his life is both historical and trans-historical. It is both human and divine Sacrifice. As divine Sacrifice, it is eternal because it is an act of the eternal High Priest. Since there is only one Sacrifice of Christ, Christ does not repeat his Sacrifice in the Holy Mass. Rather, his single and eternal Sacrifice is made present again in the celebration of the Holy Eucharist.

> **"Christ does not repeat his Sacrifice in the Holy Mass. Rather, his single and eternal Sacrifice is made present again in the celebration of the Holy Eucharist."**

Thus, the *Catechism of the Catholic Church* clearly explains this in paragraph no. 1085:

> His Paschal mystery is a real event that occurred in our history, but it is unique: all other historical events happen once, and then they pass away, swallowed up in the past. The Paschal mystery of Christ, by contrast, cannot remain only in the past, because by his death he destroyed death, and all that Christ is—all that he did and suffered for all men—participates in the divine eternity, and so transcends all times while being made present in them all. The event of the Cross and Resurrection *abides* and draws everything toward life.

Essentially included in the understanding of the one single Sacrifice of Christ is the sacrificial life of Christians who struggle to follow Christ's life of free and voluntary obedience to the Father. Saint Paul says, "Offer your bodies as a living sacrifice, holy and pleasing to God, your spiritual worship"

(*Rom* 12:1). Father Robert J. Daly, S.J., asserts that it is the dominant New Testament idea "that the life and activity of Christian people are themselves the sacrifice which they offer" (Daly, 1978, 133-134). This is eloquently elaborated by the universal Catechism in these words:

> In the Eucharist the sacrifice of Christ becomes also the sacrifice of the members of his Body. The lives of the faithful, their praise, sufferings, prayer, and work, are united with those of Christ and with his total offering, and so acquire a new value. Christ's sacrifice present on the altar makes it possible for all generations of Christians to be united with his offering (*CCC* 1368).

Conclusion

Jesus says that we are to worship God "in Spirit and truth" (*Jn* 4:24). The spiritual and doctrinal dimensions of the Holy Mass emerge as the most outstanding features of the new English translation of the Roman Missal. The emphasis on the inner disposition of the participants become evident not only in the use of a more transcendent vocabulary, but also in the rubrics on silence, striking one's breast during the *Confiteor,* and making a profound bow or genuflection in the incarnation part of the *Credo.*

By deciding for a more literal translation of the Latin texts, the Church attempts to preserve and guard the doctrinal contents of our faith as expressed in the prayers and responses of the Holy Mass. At the same time, it has been shown that the whole Mass is permeated with words from the Sacred Scriptures, either as direct quotes or indirect references. Indeed, "the prayers, collects, and liturgical songs are scriptural in their inspiration and their force, and it is from the scriptures that actions and signs derive their meaning" (*CSL* 24).

In their evaluation of Vatican II in 1985, the Extraordinary Synod of Bishops stated: "The liturgical renewal is the most visible fruit of the whole conciliar effort" (http://www.ewtn.com/library/CURIA/SYNFINAL.HTM). The third typical edition of *The Roman Missal* marks a new era of liturgical renewal in the twenty-first century. It is too early to tell whether the new English translation would be as successful as the first wave of liturgical renewal after Vatican II. It is generally accepted that the new English translation of *The Roman Missal* has its weaknesses. That is why it has not been spared from criticisms (cf. Trautman, 2010, 455-472).

However, through catechesis we begin to understand the new words and through constant use we get acquainted with them. They cease to be strange to us. Let us remember that every change is difficult. But every change is also an opportunity. With positive attitude and open heart, we will recapture "the essential aspects of the liturgical vision of Vatican II. This providential moment can allow the Holy Spirit to lead and guide us, and permit the grace of Christ to transform us" (Dunn, 2012, 349).

Appendices

A. Prayers before Mass
(From *The Roman Missal*, 1481-1484)

Prayer of Saint Ambrose

I draw near, loving Lord Jesus Christ, / to the table of your most delightful banquet / in fear and trembling, / a sinner, presuming not upon my own merits, / but trusting rather in your goodness and mercy. / I have a heart and body defiled by my many offenses, / a mind and tongue / over which I have kept no good watch. / Therefore, O loving God, O awesome Majesty, / I turn in my misery, caught in snares, / to you the fountain of mercy, / hastening to you for healing, / flying to you for protection; / and while I do not look forward to having you as Judge, / I long to have you as Savior. / To you, O Lord, I display my wounds, / to you I uncover my shame. / I am aware of my many and great sins, / for which I fear, / but I hope in your mercies, / which are without number. / Look upon me, then, with eyes of mercy, / Lord Jesus Christ, eternal King, / God and Man, crucified for mankind. / Listen to me, as I place my hope in you, / have pity on me, full of miseries and sins, / you, who will never cease / to let the fountain of compassion flow. / Hail, O Saving Victim, / offered for me and for the whole human race / on the wood of the Cross. / Hail, O noble and precious Blood, / flowing from the wounds / of Jesus Christ, my crucified Lord, / and washing away the sins of all the world. / Remember, Lord, your creature, / whom you redeemed by your Blood. / I am repentant of my sins, / I desire to put right what I have done. / Take from me, therefore, most merciful Father, / all my iniquities and sins, / so that, purified in mind and body, / I may worthily taste the Holy of Holies. / And grant that this sacred foretaste / of your Body and Blood / which I, though unworthy, intend to receive, / may be the remission of my sins, / the perfect cleansing of my faults, / the banishment of shameful thoughts, / and the rebirth of right sentiments; / and may it encourage / a wholesome and effective performance / of deeds pleasing to you / and be a most firm defense of body and soul / against the snares of my enemies. / Amen.

Prayer of Saint Thomas Aquinas

Almighty eternal God, / behold, I come to the Sacrament / of your Only Begotten Son, / our Lord Jesus Christ, / as one sick to the physician of life, / as one unclean to the fountain of mercy, / as one blind to the light of eternal brightness, / as one poor and needy to the Lord of heaven and earth. / I ask, therefore, for the abundance of your immense generosity, / that you may graciously cure my sickness, / wash away my defilement, / give light to my blindness, / enrich my poverty, / clothe my nakedness, / so that I may receive the bread of Angels, / the King of kings and Lord of lords, / with such reverence and humility, / such contrition and devotion, / such purity and faith, / such purpose and intention / as are conducive to the salvation of my soul. / Grant, I pray, that I may receive / not only the Sacrament of the Lord's Body and Blood, / but also the reality and power of the Sacrament. / O most gentle God, / grant that I may so receive / the Body of your Only Begotten Son our Lord Jesus Christ, / which he took from the Virgin Mary, / that I may be made worthy to be incorporated into his Mystical Body / and to be counted among its members. / O most loving Father, / grant that I may at last gaze for ever / upon the unveiled face of your beloved Son, / whom I, a wayfarer, / propose to receive now veiled under these species: / Who lives and reigns with you for ever and ever. / Amen.

Prayer to the Blessed Virgin Mary

O most blessed Virgin Mary, / Mother of tenderness and mercy, / I, a miserable and unworthy sinner, / fly to you with all the affection of my heart, / and I beseech your motherly love, / that, as you stood by your most dear Son, / while he hung on the Cross, / so, in your kindness, / you may be pleased to stand by me, a poor sinner, / and all Priests who today are offering the Sacrifice / here and throughout the entire holy Church, / so that with your gracious help / we may offer a worthy and acceptable oblation / in the sight of the most high and undivided Trinity. / Amen.

B. **Prayers after Mass**
(From *The Roman Missal*, 1485-1490)

Prayer of Saint Thomas Aquinas

I give you thanks, / Lord, holy Father, almighty and eternal God, / who have been pleased to nourish me, / a sinner and your unworthy servant, / with the precious Body and Blood / of your Son, our Lord Jesus Christ: / this through no merits of mine, / but due solely to the graciousness of your mercy. /

And I pray that this Holy Communion / may not be for me an offense to be punished, / but a saving plea for forgiveness. / May it be for me the armor of faith, / and the shield of good will. / May it cancel my faults, / destroy concupiscense and carnal passion, / increase charity and patience, humility and obedience / and all the virtues. / May it be a firm defense against the snares of all my enemies, / both visible and invisible, / the complete calming of my impulses, / both of the flesh and of the spirit, / a firm adherence to you, the one true God, / and the joyful completion of my life's course. /

And I beseech you to lead me, a sinner, / to that banquet beyond all telling, / where with your Son and the Holy Spirit / you are the true light of your Saints,/ fullness of satisfied desire, eternal gladness, / consummate delight and perfect happiness. / Through Christ our Lord. / Amen.

Prayer to the Most Holy Redeemer

Soul of Christ, sanctify me. / Body of Christ, save me. / Blood of Christ, embolden me. / Water from the side of Christ, wash me. / Passion of Christ, strengthen me. / O good Jesus, hear me. / Within your wounds hide me. / Never permit me to be parted from you. / From the evil Enemy defend me. / At the hour of my death call me / and bid me come to you, / that with your Saints I may praise you / for age upon age. / Amen.

Prayer of Self-Offering

Receive, Lord, my entire freedom. / Accept the whole of my memory, / my intellect and my will. / Whatever I have or possess, / it was you who gave it to me; / I restore it to you in full, / and I surrender it completely / to the guidance of your will. / Give me only love of you / together with your grace, / and I am rich enough / and ask for nothing more. / Amen.

Prayer to Our Lord
Jesus Christ Crucified

Behold, O good and loving Jesus, / that I cast myself on my knees before you / and, with the greatest fervor of spirit, / I pray and beseech you to instill into my heart / ardent sentiments of faith, hope and charity, / with true repentance for my sins / and a most firm purpose of amendment. / With deep affection and sorrow / I ponder intimately / and contemplate in my mind your five wounds, / having before my eyes what the prophet David / had already put in your mouth about yourself, O good Jesus: / They have pierced my hands and feet; / they have numbered all my bones (*Ps 21: 17-18*).

The Universal Prayer Attributed
to Pope Clement XI

I believe, O Lord, but may I believe more firmly; / I hope, but may I hope more securely; / I love, but may I love more ardently; / I sorrow, but may I sorrow more deeply. /

I adore you as my first beginning; / I long for you as my last end; / I praise you as my constant benefactor; / I invoke you as my gracious protector. /

By your wisdom direct me, / by your righteousness restrain me, / by your indulgence console me, / by your power protect me. /

I offer you, Lord, my thoughts to be directed to you, / my words, to be about you, / my deeds, to respect your will, / my trials, to be endured for you. /

I will whatever you will, / I will it because you will it, / I will it in the way you will it, / I will it for as long as you will it. /

Lord, enlighten my understanding, I pray: / arouse my will, / cleanse my heart, / sanctify my soul. /

May I weep for past sins, / repel future temptations, correct evil inclinations, / nurture appropriate virtues. /

Give me, good God, / love for you, hatred for myself, / zeal for my neighbor, contempt for the world. /

May I strive to obey superiors, / to help those dependent on me, / to have care for my friends, / forgiveness for my enemies. /

May I conquer sensuality by austerity, / avarice by generosity, / anger by gentleness, / lukewarmness by fervor. /

Render me prudent in planning, / steadfast in dangers, / patient in adversity, / humble in prosperity. /

Make me, O Lord, attentive at prayer, / moderate at meals, / diligent in work, / steadfast in intent. /

May I be careful to maintain interior innocence, / outward modesty, / exemplary behavior, / a regular life. /

May I be always watchful in subduing nature, / in nourishing grace, / in observing your law, / in winning salvation. /

May I learn from you / how precarious are earthly things, / how great divine things, / how fleeting is time, / how lasting things eternal. /

Grant that I may prepare for death, / fear judgment, / free hell, / gain paradise. / Through Christ our Lord. / Amen.

Prayer to the Blessed Virgin Mary

O Mary, Virgin and Mother most holy, / behold, I have received your most dear Son, / whom you conceived in your immaculate womb, / brought forth, nursed and embraced most tenderly. / Behold him at whose sight / you used to rejoice and be filled with all delight; / him whom, humbly and lovingly, / once again I present / and offer him to you / to be clasped in your arms, / to be loved by your heart, / and to be offered up to the Most Holy Trinity / as the supreme worship of adoration, / for your own honor and glory / and for my needs and for those of the whole world. / I ask you therefore, most loving Mother: / entreat for me the forgiveness of all my sins / and, in abundant measure, the grace / of serving him in the future more faithfully, / and at the last, final grace, / so that with you I may praise him / for all the ages of ages. / Amen.

Hail, Mary, full of grace, the Lord is with you; / blessed are you among women, / and blessed is the fruit of your womb, Jesus./ Holy Mary, Mother of God, / pray for us sinners / now and at the hour of our death. / Amen.

Bibliography

Primary Sources: Liturgical Books and Church Documents

Benedict XVI. Address to a group of Bishops from the United States of America on their *Ad limina* visit, December 4, 1993. Retrieved January 17, 2012 from the World Wide Web: http://www.vatican.va/holy_father/john_ paul_ii/speeches/1993/december/documents/ hf_jp-ii_spe_19931204_california-ad-limina_en.html.

_____. Apostolic Letter "Motu Proprio data" *Porta Fidei* for the Indiction of the Year of Faith, October 11, 2011. Retrieved December 12, 2012 from the World Wide Web: http://www.vatican.va/holy_father/ benedict_xvi/motu_proprio/documents/hf_ben-xvi_ motu-proprio_20111011_porta-fidei_en.html.

_____. *God is Love (Deus Caritas Est)*. December 25, 2005. Vatican City: Libreria Editrice Vaticana, 2006. Washington, D.C., United States Conference of Catholic Bishops, February 2006. Also available at the World Wide Web retrieved January 17, 2012: http://www.vatican.va/ holy_father/benedict_xvi/encyclicals/documents/ hf_ben-xvi_enc_20051225_deus-caritas-est_en.html.

_____. *The Sacrament of Charity (Sacramentum Caritatis)*. February 22, 2007. Vatican City: Libreria Editrice Vaticana, 2007. Washington, D.C., United States Conference of Catholic Bishops, March 2007. Also available at the World Wide Web retrieved January 17, 2012: http://www.vatican.va/holy_father/ benedict_xvi/apost_exhortations/documents/ hf_ben-xvi_exh_20070222_sacramentum-caritatis_ en.html.

_____. *Verbum Domini*. September 30, 2010. Retrieved January 12, 2012 from the World Wide Web: http://www.vatican.va/holy_father/ benedict_xvi/apost_exhortations/documents/ hf_ben-xvi_exh_20100930_verbum-domini_en.html.

Catechism of the Catholic Church. Definitive edition. Based on the Latin "Editio Typica." Retrieved January 17, 2012 from the World Wide Web: http://www. vatican.va/archive/ENG0015/INDEX.HTM.

Congregation for Divine Worship and the Discipline of the Sacraments. *Liturgiam authenticam*, March 28, 2001. Retrieved January 17, 2012 from the World

Wide Web: http://www.vatican.va/roman_curia/congregations/ccdds/documents/rc_con_ccdds_doc_20010507_liturgiam-authenticam_en.html.

Consilium for Implementing the Constitution on the Sacred Liturgy. *Comme le prevoit*. January 25, 1969. Retrieved January 17, 2012 from the World Wide Web: http://www.ewtn.com/library/CURIA/CONSLEPR.HTM.

Federation of Diocesan Liturgical Commissions. *With One Voice: Translation and Implementation of the Third Edition of the Roman Missal*. Washington, D.C.: October 2010.

The Final Report of the 1985 Extraordinary Synod. Retrieved July 8, 2012 from the World Wide Web: http://www.ewtn.com/library/CURIA/SYNFINAL.HTM.

Francis. Angelus Message of Pope Francis on May 26, 2013. Retrieved May 30, 2013 from the World Wide Web: http://www.vatican.va/holy_father/francesco/angelus/2013/documents/papa-francesco_angelus_20130526_en.html.

_____. Homily of Pope Francis for Corpus Christi, May 30, 2013. Retrieved May 30, 2013 from the World Wide Web: http://www.news.va/en/news/pope-homily-for-corpus-christi-full-text.

_____. Homily of Pope Francis on the Solemnity of Pentecost on May 19, 2013. Retrieved May 30, 2013 from the World Wide Web: http://www.vatican.va/holy_father/francesco/homilies/2013/documents/papa-francesco_20130519_omelia-pentecoste_en.html.

_____. Homily of Pope Francis at the Basilica of Saint Paul Outside-the-Walls Third Sunday of Easter on April 14, 2013. Retrieved May 30, 2013 from the World Wide Web: http://www.vatican.va/holy_father/francesco/homilies/2013/documents/papa-francesco_20130414_omelia-basilica-san-paolo_en.html.

_____. Pope Francis' Message to the German National Eucharistic Congress, June 9, 2013. Retrieved June 12, 2013 from the World Wide Web: http://www.zenit.org/en/articles/pope-francis-message-to-the-german-national-eucharistic-congress.

International Commission on English in the Liturgy, Inc. *The Roman Missal*. Collegeville, Minnesota: Liturgical Press, 2011.

_____. *Documents on the Liturgy, 1963-1979: Conciliar, Papal, and Curial Texts*. Ed. and trans. Thomas C. O'Brien. Collegeville, Minnesota: Liturgical Press, 1982.

John Paul II. *Dies Domini*. May 31, 1998. Retrieved from the World Wide Web January 17, 2012: http://www.vatican.va/holy_father/john_paul_ii/apost_letters/documents/hf_jp-ii_apl_05071998_dies-domini_en.html.

_____. *Ecclesia de Eucharistia*. April 17, 2003. Retrieved January 17, 2012 from the World Wide Web: http://www.vatican.va/holy_father/special_features/encyclicals/documents/hf_jp-ii_enc_20030417_ecclesia_eucharistia_en.html.

New American Bible. Revised Edition. Confraternity of Christian Doctrine, Inc., Washington, DC: 2010, 1991, 1986, 1970.

"Observations on the English-language Translation of the Roman Missal." Prot. n. 429/02/L. Posted by the National Catholic Reporter on May 16, 2002 at: http://ncronline.org/NCR_Online/documents/observations.htm.

Press release of the Vox Clara Committee regarding matters of liturgical translations of Latin liturgical texts into the English language (April 28-29, 2010). Retrieved August 17, 2010 from the World Wide Web: http://www.vatican.va/roman_curia/congregations/ccdds/documents/rc_con_ccdds_doc_20100428_press-release-vc_en.html.

The Sacramentary. New York: Catholic Book Publishing Co., 1974.

Second Vatican Ecumenical Council, Constitution on the Sacred Liturgy *Sacrosanctum Concilium.* December 4, 1963. Retrieved January 17, 2012 from the World Wide Web: http://www.vatican.va/archive/hist_councils/ii_vatican_council/documents/vat-ii_const_19631204_sacrosanctum-concilium_en.html.

The Voice of the Church: A Forum on Liturgical Translation. Washington, D.C.: United States Catholic Conference, 2001.

United States Conference of Catholic Bishops. "And With Your Spirit." Retrieved January 17, 2012 from the World Wide Web: http://old.usccb.org/romanmissal/translating_notes.shtml.

Secondary Sources:
Books and Articles

Chupungco, O.S.B., Anscar J., ed. *The Eucharist. Handbook for Liturgical Studies. Volume III.* Collegeville, Minnesota: The Liturgical Press, 1999.

_____. *Liturgies of the Future: The Process and Methods of Inculturation*. Mahwah, NJ: Paulist Press, 1989.

_____. *The New English Translation of the Roman Missal: A Catechetical Primer.* Manila: Archdiocesan Liturgical Commission, 2011.

Daly, Robert J. *The Origins of the Christian Doctrine of Sacrifice*. Philadelphia, 1978.

Defarrari, Trans. Roy H. Cyprian, "The Lord's Prayer," 31. *Fathers of the Church: A New Translation.* Vol. 36. New York: Fathers of the Church, Inc., 1958, 153-154. See *CCL* 3A:109.

Dunn, Brian. "*Sacrosanctum concilium* and the Call to Holiness." *Worship*. Vol. 86, Number 4. Collegeville, Minnesota: Liturgical Press, July 2012, 338-365.

Foley, Edward. *From Age to Age: How Christians Have Celebrated the Eucharist.* Revised and Expanded Edition. Collegeville: The Liturgical Press, 2008.

Foley, Edward, Nathan D. Mitchell, and Joanne M. Pierce, eds. *A Commentary on the General Instruction of the Roman Missal.* Collegeville, Minnesota: Liturgical Press, 2007.

Foley, Edward, John F. Baldovin, Mary Collins, and Joanne M. Pierce, eds. *A Commentary on the Order of Mass of the Roman Missal.* Collegeville, Minnesota: Liturgical Press, 2011.

Francis, C.S.V., Mark R. and Keith F. Pecklers, S.J., eds. *Liturgy for the New Millennium: A Commentary on the Revised Sacramentary: Essays in Honor of Anscar J. Chupungco, O.S.B.* Collegeville, Minnesota: The Liturgical Press, 2000.

Hudock, Barry. *The Eucharistic Prayer: A User's Guide.* Collegeville, Minnesota: Liturgical Press, 2010.

Johnson, Lawrence J. *The Mystery of Faith: A Study of the Structural Elements of the Order of the Mass.* Washington, D.C.: Federation of Diocesan Liturgical

Commissions, first edition, 1981; revised edition, 2006.

Jungmann, Joseph A. *The Mass of the Roman Rite: Its Origins and Development.* 2 vols. Originally published as *Missarum Sollemnia: eine genetishe ekrlarung der romischen Messe.* Trans. by Francis Brunner. New York: Benzinger Brothers, 1951. Replica edition 1986 by Chrristian Classics, Inc., Westminster, Maryland.

Lewis, C.S. *Mere Christianity.* New York: Walker and Company, 1987.

Magee, Michael K. "The Liturgical Translation of the Response '*Et cum spiritu tuo*'". *Communio.* 29, Spring 2002, 152-171.

Mahony, Cardinal Roger. *Gather Faithfully Together: Guide for Sunday Mass.* Chicago, IL: Liturgy Training Publications, 1997.

Mazza, Enrico. *The Eucharistic Prayers of the Roman Rite.* Trans. Matthew J.
O'Connell. New York: Pueblo/Collegeville: The Liturgical Press, 1986.

_____. *The Origins of the Eucharistic Prayer.* Trans. Ronald Lane.
Collegeville: The Liturgical Press, 1995.

Orbos, Fr. Jerry M., SVD. *Just a Moment: 365 Anecdotes and Reflections I'ved Shared through the*

Years. Quezon City, Philippines: Logos Publications, Inc., 2007.

Pecklers, S.J., Keith F. *Dynamic Equivalence: The Living Language of Christian Worship.* Collegeville, Minnesota: The Liturgical Press, 2003.

Ratzinger, Joseph. Pope Benedict XVI. *Jesus of Nazareth: From the Baptism in the Jordan to the Transfiguration.* Trans. Adrian J. Walker. New York: Doubleday, 2007.

_____. *Jesus of Nazareth. Part Two: Holy Week. From the Entrance into Jerusalem to the Resurrection.* San Francisco: Ignatius Press, 2011.

Ratzinger, Joseph Cardinal. *Called to Communion: Understanding the Church Today.* Trans. Adrian Walker. San Francisco: Ignatius Press, 1996. The title of the German original: *Zur Gemeinschaft gerufen: Kirche heute verstehen.* Second edition. Freiburg im Breisgau: Herder, 1991.

_____. *God is Near Us: The Eucharist, the Heart of Life.* Eds. Stephan Otto Horn and Vinzenz Pfnür. Trans. Henry Taylor. San Francisco: Ignatius Press, 2003. The title of the German original: *Gott ist uns nah. Eucharistie: Mitte des Lebens.* Augsburg, Sankt Ulrich Verlar, 2001.

Rustia, Teo S. *Rx Prayer: How Prayer Always Heals.* No place and date of publication.

Suerte Felipe, Virgilio T.J. *The Lord's Supper, Eucharist, Mass . . . What's In A Name? The Names of the Eucharist in the 2002 GIRM.* Indiana, USA: Author House, 2010.

_____. "And With Your Spirit (And Also With You)." *Boletin Eclesiastico de Filipinas.* Vol. LXXXVIII, No. 892. Manila: Ecclesiastical Publications Office, University of Santo Tomas. September-October 2012, 483-500.

Suggested websites on the new Roman Missal:

http://old.usccb.org/romanmissal/. Posted by the U.S. Bishops Committee on Divine Worship. This is the best site for official information regarding the new *Roman Missal*.

https://secure.fdlc.org/. Posted by the Federation of Diocesan Liturgical Commissions representing Roman Catholic Diocesan Offices of Worship and Liturgical Commissions throughout the United States.

http://www.davenportdiocese.org/lit/litromanmissal.htm. Posted by the Diocese of Davenport providing a wide range of additional links and resources on the new *Roman Missal*.

Trautman, Donald W. "The Language of the New Missal in Light of the Constitution on the Sacred Liturgy." *The Jurist*. 70, 2010, 455-472.

Turner, Paul. *Revised Roman Missal: Understanding the Revised Mass Texts Leader's Edition.* Chicago: Archdiocese of Chicago, Liturgy Training Publications, 2010.

_____. *Understanding the Revised Mass Texts.* Chicago: Archdiocese of Chicago, Liturgy Training Publications, 2010.

_____. *At the Supper of the Lamb: A Pastoral and Theological Commentary on the Mass.* Chicago: Archdiocese of Chicago, Liturgy Training Publications, 2011.

_____. *Let Us Pray: A Guide to the Rubrics of Sunday Mass. Updated to Conform with the Revised English Translation of The Roman Missal.* Collegeville, Minnesota: Liturgical Press, 2012.

Tuzik, Robert L., ed. *Lift Up Your Hearts: A Pastoral, Theological, and Historical Survey of the Third Typical Edition of The Roman Missal.* Chicago: Archdiocese of Chicago, Liturgy Training Publications, 2011.